This is an excel[...] [...] lived during the Depression days. Older people will remember these times. *Sharecropping in North Louisiana* is a good source of history and would be a great book to have in the elementary grades.

George Ann Harvill, Retired
Elementary Teacher, Arkansas

Sharecropping in North Louisiana is a good study of a sharecropper's life and a good study of a southern farmer's life. It is a well-written book, which I enjoyed very much.

Ted Pollard, M.D., Retired,
Age 85, Louisiana

This is a very interesting book with many details of the Depression era. I recommend this book to young people. History comes alive in *Sharecropping in North Louisiana*.

Maigyne Edge, Student, Age 14
Chidester, Arkansas

While reading *Sharecropping in North Louisiana* I felt like I was part of the family, because I also grew up a sharecropper's daughter. It was exciting to remember my own experiences of that era. I urge everyone to discuss their family history with older family members before it is too late. Being the last survivor in our family, I regret that I failed to do so.

Eunice Platt, Camden, Arkansas
Retired Business Woman

Sharecropping in North Louisiana records many interesting events of this poor family during the Depression era. The family "made do with what they had," which is a good philosophy for life that I would connect to the teachings of Scripture. It is clear that Lillian's faith in Christ is very real and that she is very secure in her faith.

Dr. Larry G. Owen, Sr., Camden, Arkansas
Doctor of Practical Ministry in Theology

This book is terrific! *Sharecropping in North Louisiana* tells of the difficulties some people experienced growing up in the twentieth century. It tells how one family made it through the troublesome times of that era.

Jessica Walter, Eleventh Grader
Victory Christian School
Camden, Arkansas

The authors of *Sharecropping in North Louisiana* tell how the family members overcame tough times. Even through hard times, their lives reflected how they trusted God to get them through it all. This is an excellent book, which has taught me a lot of good things that I can apply to my life today. I would highly recommend it to anyone as a very educational book.

Jordan Mahaffey, Eleventh Grader
Camden Christian Academy
Camden, Arkansas

This book gives a good portrayal of family life during the Great Depression. *Sharecropping in North Louisiana* will help the reader truly appreciate the courage and heart of our ancestors. I never encountered a dull moment. It is an excellent read.

Barrett Burger, Tenth Grader
Camden Christian Academy

To Mary Hislop
        Perraton

    God Bless
        You   12-13-08

SHARECROPPING IN
NORTH LOUISIANA

Lillian Duff

Linda Niemeir

LILLIAN LAIRD DUFF
&
LINDA DUFF NIEMEIR

SHARECROPPING IN NORTH LOUISIANA

A FAMILY'S STRUGGLE THROUGH THE GREAT DEPRESSION

TATE PUBLISHING & *Enterprises*

Published by Tate Publishing & Enterprises, LLC
127 E. Trade Center Terrace | Mustang, Oklahoma 73064 USA
1.888.361.9473 | www.tatepublishing.com

Tate Publishing is committed to excellence in the publishing industry. The company reflects the philosophy established by the founders, based on Psalm 68:11,
"The Lord gave the word and great was the company of those who published it."

Book design copyright © 2008 by Tate Publishing, LLC. All rights reserved.
Cover design by Nathan Harmony
Interior design by Stephanie Woloszyn

Published in the United States of America

ISBN: 978-1-60604-913-6
1. General Interest: Literature & the Arts: Essays & Memoirs
2. Biography & Autobiography: Historical: U.S. (OR) Personal Memoir
08.08.06

DEDICATION

These written words are dedicated to the memory of Eliza Flora Judy Laird, beloved mother and grandmother, who lived through those rough times. She raised her children in a loving environment, teaching them by example to love God, love one another, and do their best to live their own lives in a way that would honor their heavenly father as well as their earthly parents.

One of her favorite songs was "Let Others See Jesus in You."

—*Lillian Laird Duff and Linda Duff Niemeir*

A Few Words about My Parents

Daddy did not have the even temperament that Mama had, but he was a very hard worker. He did not always make the wisest decisions but did what he thought was best at the time. He had quite a few skills and was always willing to help others. He was a good barber but was not a licensed one. Everywhere we lived he swapped haircuts with someone else in the community who cut hair and cut friends' hair without ever charging.

My mother was kindhearted, patient, thoughtful, and non-complaining. She practiced the Golden Rule and was loved by all who knew her. She was a hard worker and a Christian who raised her children and taught her grandchildren those same principles by which she lived. She did not believe anything should be wasted if it could be useful to anyone. I did not inherit her even temperament, and as hard as I try to imitate her good qualities, I never seem to come close to her equal.

- Lillian Laird Duff

TABLE OF CONTENTS

FOREWORD

Overcoming Obstacles

For all who want a true account of a sharecropper's family life, look no further. The author gives a detailed, factual account of her life as the daughter of a sharecropper. She tells of the poverty of the family and the many moves to find better crop land. She tells of the hardships and how the frequent moves disrupted family life and school attendance.

In spite of the many moves, she always knew that her parents loved her and sacrificed to ensure the family had a place to live, food to eat, and clothes to wear. Attending school was very difficult for the children. Sometimes they had to cross the river to get to school; nevertheless, an education and success was the author's goal.

The author tells of the thrift of her mother, who canned fruits and vegetables, milked the cows, and cared for the chickens. Her mother also sewed dresses for her daughters. Even growing up as a sharecropper's daughter, she finished high school and took advanced business training so she could leave the farm and work to support herself. This made her life easier.

Later she married the man she loved and settled down to married life. The author is now a proud mother, grandmother, and great-grandmother. As you read this book, be inspired, encouraged, and blessed by the reminiscing of this remarkable Christian lady who overcame the sharecropper label and happily shares her story with others.

Etheleen M. Garrison
Retired Registered Nurse
Camden, Arkansas

INTRODUCTION

This book is being written by my mother, Lillian Laird Duff, and me, Linda Duff Niemeir. The intention is to put on paper the struggles of my mother's family during the Great Depression and WWII years. Their lives were further complicated by the fact that my grandfather was a tenant farmer, better known in those days as a sharecropper.

I grew up hearing many of the stories told about Mama's life as a child and some of those hard times she and her family endured. The stories fascinated me so much that I asked Mama if it would be okay for us to write a book telling about her life at that time so my son and grandchildren would know on a personal basis some of the history of that era.

If you are old enough to remember some of those years from the early 1900s, you are fortunate indeed and very blessed to have lived long enough to reminisce as you read our book. If you are among the younger generations reading of these years past, then you will most likely be reminded of the things you are blessed to have in your life at this time and hopefully be grateful for them. I know that I sure am.

The following paragraphs will introduce you to the members of my mother's family. The fourteen chapters of the book will tell you something of those years during the Depression and World War II and how the family coped with the hard times.

My maternal grandfather Joseph Clarence Laird was born June 28, 1899, near Sandersville, Mississippi. He was one of three children born to Susan Frances Purvis Laird and J.W. Laird. His mother died in childbirth when he was two years old, so his paternal grandmother moved into their home for a while to care for the three small children, Agnes, Erastus (Ras), and Clarence. Later Great-Grandpa Laird married Grandma Georgia, and they had ten more children. They lived near Sandersville and Ellisville, Mississippi, where Grandpa Laird grew up.

My maternal grandmother, Eliza Flora Judy, was born in Badham, Dorchester County, on August 27, 1902, in the St. George community about fifty miles from Charleston, South Carolina. Born to Sarah and Asbury Jacob Judy, she was one of seven children of whom only she and a sister, Iva, survived to adulthood. Her mother died when Grandma Eliza was only four years old.

After Great-Grandma Sarah died in 1906 at the age of thirty-eight, possibly during childbirth, Great-Grandpa Judy had to leave the two girls with various relatives while he worked out of town to make a living. He was forty at that time and eventually remarried. But when that marriage did not work out, he decided to move to Mississippi where his older sister, Emma Patrick, had moved with her husband, Henry. He packed their meager belongings of clothes, quilts, and a featherbed in three large trunks. Great-Grandpa Judy and his girls took the train from South Carolina to Mississippi.

Eliza was nine years old at that time, and Aunt Iva was twelve. They attended school in Sandersville for two years together, but Aunt Iva married at age fourteen. Grandpa Judy taught Eliza some cooking skills, but she learned more cooking and housekeeping skills from friends and neighbors. They taught her to can, quilt, embroider, and crochet. Grandma said someone was always willing to teach her if she only asked, and she was always willing to learn. She had patience and persistence in learning these new skills and put them into practice all her life.

In 1917, while at an Indian dance in Sandersville, Eliza met a tall, handsome man named Joseph Clarence Laird. They kept company occasionally until Eliza and her father moved to Louisiana in the fall of 1918. She and Clarence corresponded for two years, and then he went to Louisiana where they married on July 25, 1920, in Dorig, Louisiana. Grandpa had just had his twenty-first birthday in June, and Grandma turned eighteen in August after they married. The next day they left on a train out of Mangham, Louisiana, to return to

Sandersville, Mississippi, where Grandpa soon became employed in the lumber industry for a short time. By the next year he was farming, and it was in September 1921 that their first daughter, Eliza Josephine, was born.

In the fall of that year after the crop was gathered, they moved back to Louisiana. Grandpa had seen that the land in Louisiana was better for farming than the hill country that he had known in Mississippi. However, for some reason Grandpa moved them back to Mississippi in 1922 where he did public work in Laurel and Sandersville. It was here that their second daughter, Gladys Florine, was born in July 1923. She was healthy for a long time but became very ill when she was thirteen months old and died of dysentery in August 1924. That fall they moved back to Louisiana to the Charlie McIntosh place on Boeuf River in Richland Parish. This was the same house that Grandma Eliza was living in when she and Grandpa were married.

After their crop was gathered, they moved across the river to the Joe Harris place in Caldwell Parish in the fall of 1925. Josephine was four years old by that time. On June 22, 1926, their third daughter, Lillian Katherine, was born. Thus my mother, the storyteller of the following chapters, entered this wandering sharecropping family.

J.C. Laird, age 19

Eliza Flora Judy, 1920, age 17

Florine & Josephine, Fall 1923

SHARECROPPING

"Mama, you said your father was a sharecropper. Just what does that mean?"

Well, a sharecropper was a tenant who made his living for himself and his family on a farm even though he did not own land or a house. He was required to share certain crops with the landowner. He did not own a team of mules or any farm tools. There were people who had farms and lots of land, and they needed the land worked. Everyone benefited from sharecropping when the landlord would furnish a team, tools, and a house for the tenant. Sometimes a landowner had more than one tenant. There was a central barn and pastureland. The tenants or sharecroppers would agree to live in a house and farm a portion of the land and share the crop with the landlord at the agreed percentage. Let me say that I doubt if there are any sharecroppers today because of mechanized farming.

The houses were not very good—always unpainted and made of rough lumber. Sometimes they had no screens on the windows, and if there were, many times they did not fit tightly enough to keep the mosquitoes or flies out. We had to be careful going in and out of the doors because there were lots of flies on a farm. The screens on the windows and doors kept the chickens out of the house because chickens had free range of the yard. The chickens found some of their food by scratching in the dirt for bugs and insects. Most of the houses were not sealed at all. Sometimes the rooms were partially sealed. Many floors had cracks from old age and a lot of scrubbing. Sometimes when a tenant family moved in, they noticed the walls had been papered with newspaper by the previous tenants to help make the house warmer. The paste that had been used was made of flour and water, which attracted insects, commonly known as chinches. Today these insects are known as bedbugs. In those days all we had to use to try to get rid of them was kerosene, commonly known as coal oil. We had to scrub down the walls and get that old paper and paste off. At least the bugs did not have hiding places when the paper was removed.

I remember at least one house like that, and Mama told me about others she'd lived in that had to be cleaned in this manner, but not all of them. Some houses had batten-board walls, which means the outside walls of perpendicular planks had narrow boards covering the cracks between the wide boards. All these boards were rough lumber and not painted. They appeared very weathered and gray inside and out, very similar to what a very old barn might look like today. If we were lucky, the floorboards were made of finished lumber and had no cracks but were still unpainted. Some of our houses had floors of lumber with cracks wide enough that when scrubbed some of the scrub water would run through the cracks. Mops could not be used because the splinters would hang up the strings of the mop, so we used an old broom.

None of these houses had indoor plumbing during all the years I was at home. The wells or water pumps were outside and not always near the house. Baths were taken in washtubs near the kitchen stove in the winter and on the back porch in warm weather. In the summer we pumped the water and filled the tub, which had been placed in a sunny spot on the porch. By nighttime it was nice and warm for bathing. Then, of course, there was always the little house a short distance behind our home that held the faithful old Sears, Roebuck catalog.

During the years 1929 through 1936, our family moved every year. We would move to a place, and Daddy would make an agreement with the landowner to work the land, but he would become dissatisfied with the situation for one reason or another, thinking he could do better someplace else. He would go out walking in the fall, looking to find another place for us to live. As a young child, I did not understand why we moved so often. As I grew older I realized that Daddy was looking for better land, a better house, or better location in relation to school, church, and town. Finally, our family moved to a place in December 1936 where we stayed for eight years. Those moves were complicated by the Depression, which lasted through the 1930s and up until just before World War II. Then along came the complication of the shortages caused by the war. Life was often hard, but Mama never complained about the difficulties and hard work. Whatever needed to be done, she just did it.

When sharecropping, there would be only a verbal agreement between the farm owner and the tenants to raise the crops. Cotton and corn were the two main crops in those days in the areas where we lived. The cash crop was cotton, but corn was also important. Those were the only crops the sharecroppers were required to share with the landowner. The tenants could plant gardens, pea patches, and other crops for their personal use on a small portion of the landowner's fields. But the tenants had to agree to plant a certain amount of the cash crop to share with the landowner. Most of the time Daddy's agreement was to give half of the profits at harvest to the landowner. Sometimes sharecroppers made agreements for other amounts.

The sharecroppers worked the cotton and gathered it by hand to be taken to the cotton gin and sold. They received half of the money and the landowner the other half per their agreement. The half going to the landowner was in payment for the use of the land and house and tools and the team. The corn was also divided in half with the landlord. His half was stored in his barn. It was used to feed the mules during the wintertime and anytime they were in the barn not being used by the tenant. When the tenant had the team, working them on the farm, he had to feed the mules out of his half of the corn. If it was not used up, the balance could be used to feed any hogs or chickens he owned.

When he needed a certain kind of tool like a turning plow or a middle-buster, the tenant would have to go to the central barn. A turning plow had only one wing and turned the land in only one direction—the right-hand side. The middle buster had two wings, and it busted the land right down the middle and turned it both ways. There was a tool called a side harrow, sometimes nicknamed a gee-whiz. Another very useful tool, called a Georgia stock, had plows that could be fastened to the beam. It was probably invented in the state of Georgia, but I am not sure. The farmer could put different types of plows on the beam. It was lightweight and could be used to plow up close to the crop or in the middle with a plow called a sweep. The sweep would go just under the ground, rooting up the grass so the sun would kill the grass.

If the tenant needed to haul something, he had to go to the big barn to get a wagon. He could keep it a few days if he needed to. There were usually several wagons, depending on how big the farm was. One time we lived on a farm that was small enough that the landowner required only one tenant farmer, or sharecropper. The sharecropper could use the wagon to haul in his corn or to haul wood. The landlord usually allowed the tenant to cut wood on his land. The old timber was cut out most of the time so the new trees could grow. There were different rules, according to the landowner. Daddy used the wagon to haul his sugarcane in the fall when it was time to make syrup. We didn't always have a patch of cane but grew sugarcane as often as possible. The syrup was for our family's use, and we were not required to divide it with the landlord, though Daddy probably shared some with them.

You might wonder how all this got started. The way it seems to have gotten started is that after the War between the States was over, some of the plantations were in bad shape. Many of the buildings were run down or had been burned down by the northern army. When the men came back from the war, some of them were crippled or blind. Many of the young boys had gone to fight too, because boys as young as fourteen or fifteen were considered men. Women and children left at home during the war had a hard time taking care of the farms because there were no men left to work. After the war there were no slave hands to help because they were then free and wanted to go off on their own and be their own bosses.

Some of the freed slaves tried that for a while but saw that they could not farm on their own since they did not own land. So it became a necessity for former slaves to stay on the plantations if the landlord would let them. Farming was all they knew. Sometimes there were slave cabins still standing, and the former slaves could still live in them. The landlord or his widow and orphan children needed someone to work the land. So the former slaves lived in those little cabins and worked the land, and there was an agreement between them and the landowners. This benefited the landowners and the workers.

The workers were not always freed slaves. Some were poor white people. Some of them might have had a little farm before they had left for the war, or some might have worked for the landlord as advisors or overseers. Sometimes they were spoken of in the antebellum novels about the War between the States as poor white trash. Well, they were poor and were white, but most were good people and hard workers. The Bible says: "For ye have the poor always with you: but me ye have not always" (Matthew 26:11). Many people were poor during those years after the War between the States and also during the Depression. There were poor people then, and there are poor people now.

So the way the sharecroppers got started had to do with the landowners' need for workers and the poor workers' need for a job and a home. The landlords would allow the sharecroppers to use part of the land to grow food for their families. In this manner the sharecroppers were able to make a living. Sometimes the landowners ran small stores where the workers could make purchases for cash or put them on charge accounts. This was sometimes called standing for their furnish or needs. Both landowners and sharecroppers benefited from this arrangement when the crop was harvested and shared.

The tenants were expected to buy only necessities

and if possible to raise everything else. I don't know if everyone stuck to that, but I do know we did. We raised everything that we could possibly raise to eat, and we bought only the necessities. Our grocery list sometimes would be flour, sugar (once in a while), a little coffee, some coal oil for our lamps, tobacco for Daddy, cigarette papers for rolling his cigarettes, and occasionally a little package of rice. We all loved rice and could not grow it. Our family did not feel we were deprived; it was just the way life was for us.

FEEDING THE FAMILY

We usually raised a pea patch and ate off the patch while the peas were green. Once the peas dried, we picked them, and when they were really dry, we thrashed them. We put the peas in a strong sack, usually a cotton sack, and laid them on the ground and beat them with a board or stick. We often used an axe handle, which was flat on one end. Daddy made his own axe handles because they were more durable than the ones he could buy. He made them out of hickory and always had spares around the house.

After the peas were thrashed, the pea hulls could be sifted out. The peas were at the bottom of the vessel, and the chaff was on top. At the bottom where there was very little chaff, we could pour them from one vessel to another or onto a large piece of material, tarp, or old quilt, which we would lay on the ground. If the wind was blowing, the wind would blow away the chaff as the peas fell onto the quilt. If there was no wind, a person could use a large piece of cardboard to fan away the chaff. This process is known as winnowing, which is spoken of in the Bible in Matthew 3:12 and again in Luke 3:17. This was how we prepared our peas for use in the winter. They were dried just like the dry peas or beans we buy in the stores today. They could be washed, soaked, and cooked with a piece of smoked pork meat. Mama would make a pan of cornbread, and we usually had canned chow chow on hand. Our chow chow was made of cabbage, cucumbers, green tomatoes, peppers, and onions, all chopped and seasoned with vinegar, sugar, and salt. With a glass of milk, we had dinner or supper.

Speaking of the pork that we smoked, we were not required to share the pork that we raised for the family; however, for good relations with the landlords, my daddy always took them fresh meat when we killed the hogs. I am not sure if he took them any after it was cured; possibly if he were asking a favor of the landlord. He always shared fresh pork when we killed hogs, and the landlords seemed to always appreciate that. It had to be very cold weather, possibly freezing, at hog-killing times to cure the meat. Killing a hog in hot or warm weather would allow the meat to spoil before it was cured or smoked. Also, there would not be any flies when it was very cold. We would put it in a wooden box with a few small cracks in it and cover the meat completely with salt. The hog would have been cut up into hams, shoulders, pork-chop strips, and "middlings." The middling was the belly part of the hog, which was used to make bacon.

During the three to four weeks that the pork was in the salt box, Daddy would occasionally check to make sure there was plenty of salt. As the water from the pork melted the salt and ran out through the cracks, he would add more salt so the meat would not spoil. The salt would draw the water out of the meat, which made the meat drier and firmer and ready to be smoked.

After the salting process, Daddy took the meat out, removed the salt, and washed the meat well with warm water. Then he washed it with cold water and let it drip and patted it dry. Then everything except the pork-chop strips was hung up in our smokehouse. The pork chops that were cut from this piece of meat were eaten fresh. The smokehouse was built with a dirt floor so the meat could be hung up on wires that hung from the ceiling.

The smokehouse was built tight to keep any animals out. The wires were used in case any mice got in; they could not walk on the wires and get to the meat. We started a small fire under the meat on the dirt floor for safety precautions and let it catch up just a little bit using green hickory wood that would not blaze up but just smolder and make smoke. The smoke would drift up to the top and smoke that meat. It smelled so good! After several weeks or more, the meat would be thoroughly cured and no longer need the smoke under it. The smoked meat was left in the smokehouse until it was needed.

Of course the meat could be used at any point, but it would not have the cured, smoked taste early in the process. If we wanted it to keep until spring after it got warmer outside, it had to be thoroughly cured. Daddy would not leave it in big pieces to make sure it was cured all the way to the center, especially the loin part of the ham and certainly if we had a large hog. That was going to be our meat during the winter and into the spring, but we could not keep it too long after warm weather.

As long as we kept smoke on the meat, the flies would stay away; but there came a time when it had to be used up or it would no longer be good because we did not have refrigeration. In fact none of us in the country at that time had electricity. The bacon lasted the longest because it could be removed from the smokehouse and wrapped in brown paper and kept awhile longer. When the smoked meat was gone, we did not have meat unless we started killing the young chickens.

Mama started setting the hens just as soon as possible in the early spring so we would have meat during the summer. Eggs were plentiful all the time because we had many hens that we did not allow to set. After hens have laid eggs for a while, most breeds begin to feel the motherly instinct to reproduce. They will get a fever and remain on their nests all night instead of going to the roost with all the other chickens where they usually go at night. If Mama did not want a hen to set at that time, she would shut her in a coop with feed and water until the hen's temperature was normal. If she wanted the hen to set, she would select fifteen large eggs for setting. These eggs would be marked with a dark pencil so if another hen laid an egg in that nest, it would be easily identified for removal. The original fifteen eggs were allowed to incubate under the setting hen for three weeks, at which time they would begin to hatch. Mama learned which hens were best for brooding (raising and caring for chicks) and which were best for laying. Eggs were one of our main breakfast foods all year. We had both eggs and fried chicken often for breakfast in the summertime when vegetables were abundant for dinner and supper. We all worked hard on the farm, so the calories from carbohydrates and fats were quickly burned.

Our family had some foods that we ate regularly and other foods that we ate only on occasion. As far as the rice was concerned, when Mama and Daddy married, he knew nothing about rice; it was never purchased or served in his home when he was a child. Grandpa Laird had always kept purchases to necessities, and rice was not one. When Mama bought rice and cooked it, Daddy learned he really enjoyed it. We cooked it as often as we could afford it.

In the summertime the weevils would get in our corn, so we would have to buy cornmeal too. In the wintertime we took the corn that we raised to the grist mill to have it ground into cornmeal. Sometimes we would have it ground coarsely, and the meal could be sifted out, leaving the grits with some chaff. What went through the sifter was cornmeal used to make cornbread. Grits and chaff remained in the sifter. When it came time to cook grits, the mixture was poured into water, where the chaff floated off, leaving the grits. Of course Mama always made cornbread every day, winter and summer, for dinner and supper. We usually ate grits only in the winter. Biscuits were cooked winter and summer for breakfast.

As sharecroppers we were allowed to have milk cows. Usually there was some free range or pasture for the cows to graze together. The cows would come up near the house at night for water and to be milked and because their calves were penned up in a small pasture. We milked the cows at night and again in the morning before turning them out to pasture again. In certain areas there was no free range, and we had to keep them in a pasture. We had to have a separate pasture for the calves and cows with a good fence between them. The calves would go up to the fence to beg for their mama, who would get close to the fence, and if the calf could get its head through the fence, we would not have very much milk when it came milking time; the calf would have taken care of that.

We were also allowed and encouraged to gather in any hay or roughage of any kind that our cows could eat. We often planted clay peas, which were non-vining. When they got to a certain stage, we would pick the peas then cut the pea bushes as hay for the cows. There would be some peas still on the vines, and the cows liked them. We would also gather the blades off the corn for the cows. Sometimes we would cut off the tops after the corn stalks had dried and tie them into sheaves with a blade of the corn. When they were dried and cured, this was another type of hay the cows loved.

We also grew sweet potatoes and bedded them out to cure in the garden somewhere to save them for the winter. In northern Louisiana where we lived, the ground did not usually freeze more than a few inches deep. After digging up the potatoes from the field, Daddy would usually dig down a bed about a foot deep in a round circle about four to five feet across, tossing the dirt outside the bed. Then he laid some hay in the bed and placed the potatoes on the hay very carefully, in order not to skin them. The mound of potatoes was then covered with hay. He placed corn stalks around them to form a teepee and threw the dirt back upon the bed part of the way up. Later he would throw dirt higher, leaving a hole at the top for ventilation. I seem to remember he put a piece of tin over that hole so the rain could not pour in. Some rain would go through the hay and corn stalks, and that was fine. The potatoes were supposed to be kept damp but allowed to cure. After a while they would become cured, containing less water. Then it was time to bake them. Of course the smaller ones were best for baking, and the larger, chunky potatoes were cut up for frying, making pies, or for feeding the hogs and cows.

So with our dry peas, our tomatoes that had been canned in jars, our sweet potatoes, and our cured meat, we could eat during the wintertime without many purchases out of the store. And of course we had our eggs. In the wintertime we would feed the chickens corn, and they gathered some of their feed on the range.

We had our milk and butter and usually biscuits or grits in the morning. We had eggs with ham or bacon from the smoke house, so what more could we want? We could have the eggs any way we wanted them. In the wintertime we had lots of butter because the cows were turned into the field, and there was lots of foliage and rich stuff for them to eat. They provided lots of good, rich milk for drinking and for making butter.

Our cows were part Jersey. They gave so much milk that we had more butter than we could use and more milk than we could drink. We gave spare milk to the hogs and to the chickens. We let some of the milk sour, and we churned our own butter by hand. The soft churned butter floated on top of the buttermilk, so it was skimmed off. It was placed in a bowl and gently folded until the excess liquid separated from the butter. We drained off the liquid, lightly salted the butter, and put it in a little bowl or made a mound out of it in a saucer. The next morning it was great with biscuits and syrup, one of our favorite breakfast meals. In the summertime we took the fresh warm milk from the afternoon milking and put it in pint jars then set them in a dishpan of freshly pumped, cool water. We stirred it occasionally and changed the water several times. After a little while it was as cool as the pump water, and at suppertime it tasted almost like it came from an icebox.

We never had an icebox on the farm, but sometime in the latter part of June, for mine and Daddy's birthdays or for the Fourth of July, Daddy would go out to the highway and flag down the ice truck. He would buy a big block of ice, maybe fifty pounds, and bring it back so we could make ice cream. We would wrap the ice in an old wool blanket and old quilts and keep it in a cool place until we were ready to make the ice cream—usually the next day. Mama took milk, eggs, cream, sugar and vanilla, mixed it well, and put it in the metal container of the ice cream freezer. Then we chipped the ice and sprinkled it liberally with salt and placed it around the ice cream container, which was to be hand cranked, in the freezer. We took turns cranking the handle, and when it began to be difficult to crank, we knew it was almost ready. We all thoroughly enjoyed this treat.

When it came to Daddy's favorite breakfast foods, biscuits and syrup, sometimes he was out of luck, because we didn't always have syrup. Some years we didn't raise sugarcane, but I am not sure exactly why. Possibly it was because we had to have some seed to start, and it was not seed as you might know it. It had to be cane that had been gathered and bedded down similarly to the way we bedded down the sweet potatoes. The next spring it was dug out and laid in the rows and covered up. Each joint had an eye on it, and that was what made a new stalk of sugarcane when it came up. That was usually the source of our syrup.

If we didn't have sugarcane, we could plant sorghum

from seed (which looked similar to bird seed), but we
didn't like the taste of sorghum like some folks did.
We tried it only once. If we didn't have either one of
those, there was one alternative, but it was expensive.
That was sugar syrup. It was made by filling a pint jar
with sugar, which had to be purchased. Then we filled
the jar with boiling water. We stirred it up, and when
the sugar dissolved, the mixture was thin, but it was
also sweet. On a good hot biscuit with good butter, it
was wonderful. This was almost as good to Daddy as
regular syrup because he loved sweets.

So our family ate very well most of the time during
those hard years, but we struggled to make food
for ourselves as well as our livestock. As poor as we
were, we realized how important our cattle, hogs, and
chickens were to our livelihood. It was hard to always
maintain our livestock and move them with us, but
Daddy persisted in that endeavor.

THE FLOOD OF 1927

It was on June 22, 1926, in Caldwell Parish, that I was born. Caldwell Parish is in northern Louisiana, just south of Monroe. My sister Josephine was four years old that summer. We were living on Mr. Joe Harris's place, but in the fall of that year we moved to Mr. Henry Shipp's farm in the north end of Caldwell Parish. This was very close to Boeuf (pronounced Beff) River.

In the spring of 1927, a lot of rain fell, and the water began to rise in all rivers and tributaries of the Mississippi River. We found out later that a lot of rain had fallen in the northern states as early as the spring before and all through the year of 1926. In April and May of 1927, it became necessary for families in our area to evacuate. No one in my family realized at the time the extent of this flood, but we found out years later how it affected almost one-third of these United States.

Because I was only about ten months old when our family had to move to higher ground, I can only tell you what Mama told me about how we survived. It was a terrible thing to happen and affected hundreds of thousands of people in many states. Mama said she and Daddy watched the water rise out back in the field as it got closer and closer each morning. As the water neared the house, Mama said they began gathering crawfish in the edge of the backwater. This was her first time to eat them, and she said they were delicious. At some point they were told the water would not recede anytime soon and that folks would have to leave their farms and homes.

Daddy and Grandpa made scaffolds in the house and barn on which to place our furniture and belongings. The lumber they used for the scaffolding came from the floorboards of the house. In the barn they used them to put up tools and farm equipment above the rising water. Rafts were built for our livestock and chickens. As the water rose, the hogs were so hungry they dived through the water to uproot and eat the onions in the garden. The chickens were placed on a raft so they could be fed and kept dry. Pretty soon our cow and the hogs were also placed on a raft so they would not drown. The raft with the livestock was too heavy to float, so Daddy and Grandpa placed logs under the raft as the water rose. As the water became deeper, they placed more logs under the raft.

When it came time to leave, Daddy took us and our clothes and Mama's treadle sewing machine in a boat out to the Landerneau's landing, which was the highest point in that part of the parish. We spent the night at Mrs. Landerneau's, but Daddy went back to help Grandpa take care of the animals and help the neighbors get their animals to safety. Mama told me later that the next morning Mrs. Landerneau noticed that the damp weather was causing my hair to curl as Mama combed it down. She told Mama that if she would comb my hair up instead of down, it would curl, and indeed it did. Then Mama, Josephine, and I boarded the steamboat, which would take us to the refugee camp. That boat had fifty-two passengers and a crew. It was only a day's journey to the camp at Banks Springs just south of Columbia.

There were many tents for the families, and beds were made from blankets on bales of hay. Mama said she was told to raise her tent walls any morning possible to ensure airflow and help prevent disease. It was very hard to keep enough diapers dry in the damp weather. The Red Cross fed the people from a community kitchen. For breakfast they were given bacon, eggs, light bread, and coffee. These country folk did not appreciate the light bread because they preferred biscuits and cornbread. So, some of the men were able to bring in their cook stoves on one of their trips back from checking on their home places. This enabled the women to cook biscuits and cornbread. Mama remembered that each family was given an apple a day for the children.

At some point Daddy joined us at the camp, but Grandpa Judy stayed behind. He lived in the high part of Mr. Landerneau's empty gin house and tended to the animals by boat. He used dirt on some boards on which to build a safe cook fire. He ate a lot of rabbits that were stranded on a small bit of high ground. He also had in the beginning the English peas he had gathered from the garden before the water covered it and the eggs from our chickens. We were at the camp about a month, but Mama said we got home that summer in time to plant a late crop.

Mama and Daddy moved to Mississippi shortly after the great flood. Grandpa Judy stayed in Louisiana and kept the livestock and chickens. In 1928 and 1929, we lived in southern Mississippi near Wiggins, close to my Daddy's relatives. My earliest memory is a brief glimpse when I was about three years old. I remember being with my sister Josephine and several of our aunts, who were children like we were. Daddy had several half-sisters who were not much older than me and Josephine. We were all playing together and watching my Grandpa Laird and a neighbor pass by the house in a wagon with a lot of shiny syrup cans in the wagon bed. They were on their way to make syrup at a nearby syrup mill. In those days the sugarcane was crushed between rollers powered by a mule. I got a chance to work at a syrup mill when I was fourteen years old.

It was while my parents lived in Mississippi and I was very young that Mama planted some butter beans down the sides of the house. I was too young to remember, but she told me years later that Daddy made poles for the beans to run on and leaned them against the eaves of the house. The beans grew so tall that they ran up those poles several feet above the roof.

Daddy leaned a ladder up against the house so Mama could climb up to pick the butter beans. It is hard for me to imagine, but Mama said she stood on that roof many times picking butter beans for us to eat. There were excess beans, and she said she sold a bushel for five dollars.

Back in Louisiana after the flood, Grandpa Judy moved to the front side of the slough on the Shipp place and built a house. Mr. Shipp had given him permission to do this and to use timber from his land. Grandpa's house was made from rough lumber and had two large rooms, the front room being the kitchen/ living area with a fireplace that had a stick-and-dirt chimney. The back room was his bedroom. Naturally he built an outhouse as well. Mama told me he lived there while we were in Mississippi. After we moved back, we visited him there in the spring of 1930 where Josephine and I had our picture made with him on the front steps. I remember the house and sitting outside for the picture. I was three years old at that time, and Josephine was eight.

Josephine, age 8; Grandpa Judy, age 66; Lillian, age 3. On
the steps of the house with the stick and dirt chimney in
Spring 1930

The next memory I have is also that same year when we
lived near Baskin, which I believe is in Franklin Parish.
Daddy had a Ford Model A at this time for a while.
He was farming for a cousin of his, Lou Fuller. His
house was near ours, so Josephine and I had cousins to
play with. I remember that I had shoulder length, curly
hair. We did not have a hair brush, and my hair tangled
easily. It hung in ringlets around my face and had to be
combed every day. I was tender-headed, so combing it
was a bad job.

Lillian with hair in ringlets

In the early spring of 1930, out in front of our house, there were thousands of tiny wildflowers blooming. Josephine and I would sit in the yard and play amidst those flowers for hours. Shortly afterward I became ill, and Mama said my breathing was so hard it rattled the bed springs. She was afraid I had pneumonia, which was very serious in those days. Daddy sent for a doctor, who came and said he thought I had an illness related to having played among the flowers. I eventually recovered, but that was the last of my playing in the wildflowers. I remember that Mama cut my hair that summer to a more manageable length to save time for her and tears for me.

Lillian & Josephine, Spring 1930

I also remember having a picture taken with my cousin Louis Fuller, who was about my same age, that summer of 1930. I think his birthday was in June, as was mine, but I don't know which of us was older. Our birthdays were very close together; we were four years old at the time.

I don't remember much else at that age, but one thing comes to my mind about some wild hogs that ran in the woods near our house just outside Baskin. They would come up around the house sometimes, and there was a sow that had quite a few little pigs—maybe as many as six. She was hungry and wild, and she was eating her piglets. I don't know what made her do that. My mother hemmed one of those little pigs in against the garden fence.

Mama sow went on her way, and I don't know what happened to her, but we kept that little pig. She still had a wild nature, but Mama kept her for several years. I do remember that she grew into a long-bodied sow. She was black with a white stripe around her middle. That is usually called a Listed Hampshire, I believe. In some places people turned their cows and hogs out into the woods. This was called free range, so the fields had to be fenced to keep the wild hogs out of the crops. I suppose that is the way it was there, and why she was running wild.

I remember Mama catching that little pig, and she probably fed it milk and scraps from the table. That was the start of our hogs that we had for a number of years. I think we were milking one of cousin Lou's cows at the time. That hog later had big litters of pigs for several years after she was grown. Four years later we took a picture of her with one of her many litters. I don't remember what happened to her, but she had the wild nature that her mama had. If a chicken got in her pen or she chased one up in the corner of a fence or anywhere, she would eat it. To her that was just food.

Lillian with mama sow & little pigs

A Move to Richland Parish

We moved about Christmastime in 1930 to the Hubert Thompson place in Richland Parish. I remember that the first night we stopped by the landlord's house the children there had toys I had never seen before. Some were pull toys and one was a tricycle. I don't know if I got a chance to ride it, but it sure did look fancy to me. We were very poor, and I had never had anything like that because times were hard. This was not long after the big stock market crash.

This move required that Josephine walk a ways to school that January in 1931—at least a mile on a gravel road. Josephine was nine, and I was four and one-half years old. It was lonesome, and she didn't know anybody. Mama went to talk to the teacher, Mrs. Landerneau. I suppose Mama had to walk there too, which was the only way she had of going anywhere. Mama enrolled Josephine in school, and the teacher suggested that Mama send me to school also. Mrs. Landerneau suggested that I come to school with Josephine so she would not be lonesome walking on that road by herself. This was a good arrangement for Mama as well, because it freed up her time for work on the farm. At least there was not much danger in those days. It was not like times are now.

I was so young at that time, and even though the teacher could not enroll me in school at that age, she wanted me to attend classes. This was a small country school, and the teacher thought it would help her keep her school if she had more students attending. A local boy, Stanley Douciere, also attended school with his older brother that year, so that must have been a common practice. The school was located near the Douciere Plantation, so the school was called Douciere School. It turned out that Mama had gone to that very school when she was a teenager, when she lived farther down the river with Grandpa Judy, before she married.

Josephine and I started to school, but I didn't have any books. Mama fixed us both a lunch, and we went to that little one-room school. I heard the other children in the room as they interacted with Mrs. Landerneau; at the time I think we had first through third grades only. It was not long before I began enjoying looking at Josephine's school books. She had some books she had used in Mississippi. One of them was a little blue reader and one a little brown reader. I liked looking at those books and looked forward to the time that I would learn to read, but in the meantime I pretended to read. Occasionally someone would give us some funny papers, so I would just make up the words. Some of the words were just jabber, but that was how I pretended to read.

As I sat in the class, I learned to listen, and I had a pretty good memory for things. Soon I could repeat some of the little poems. I loved poems and anything that rhymed. Because I wanted to read and to rhyme things, I would try to make a rhyme and take a word like bat and see how many words I could make that sounded like bat…and just try to make words that sounded alike. I especially liked poems by Robert Lewis Stevenson. Mama also enjoyed poems and had memorized many from her school days. I continued going to school with Josephine that year but was not officially enrolled in the first grade until the fall session after I turned five.

In 1931 Grandpa Judy bought a cow for us, and we named her Lucy. Lucy gave us a calf every year and helped us get a start of cattle. Grandpa paid fifty dollars for her because she was reputed to be a very good milk cow. That was a large sum of money at that time. Grandpa was a very thrifty man, but this was probably a big portion of his savings. Lucy was a very good milk cow but was very peculiar. She didn't like men to be around her, possibly because a man might have chased her at some point. She didn't like dogs either, so all dogs and men kept their distance while she was being milked. She kicked when she was milked, so we had to use anti-kickers. We put feed out on a shelf in the milking chute and put sticks behind her to keep her in. There was a place on the right side for the milker to squat. Before milking we placed the anti-kickers, which were made of metal, on her back knee joints and fastened them together with a rope so she had very little movement of her hind feet. This allowed Mama to milk her safely. Lucy would try to kick but could not. She had to be milked this way every morning and night, but she lived up to her reputation as a good milk cow and was well worth the trouble.

At this time we lived very close to Boeuf River, and Daddy would gig for fish. This involved spearing the fish with a three-pointed gig along the riverbank at night. He used a carbide light to see the fish as they came up close to the bank to feed. The fish he caught were usually catfish, and one time he caught a really big one, possibly thirty pounds.

At the end of 1931, we moved across the river to Mr. Jasper Harrell's place. Our school then would have been in Caldwell Parish (Girod School), but Mama wanted us to finish the year out at Dosciere School. She wrote to the school superintendent in Caldwell Parish and received permission for us to continue in school across the river in Richland Parish. So we continued to go to school at Dosciere School after we moved. Mama would take us across the river every morning in a boat. She could not swim, and neither could we, nor did we have life jackets. It was just one of those things, which was the best we could do.

That spring of 1932, we had lots of rain, and the river overflowed its banks again. Some people began to wonder if we might have another flood like the one in 1927. Fortunately, we did not. We had to paddle through the woods almost a mile on the overflow side in the mornings before we got to the deep part of the river to cross. In the afternoons Mama met us on the deep side, and we made the return trip. She put us across every day and met us after school and brought us home in that wooden paddle boat. Mama told us to be careful to sit still, and we did. She knew this was dangerous, but she just had no alternative. This crossing must have been one of the designated river crossings along the Boeuf River. The boat was left on the Caldwell Parish side for people to get to Richland Parish, possibly to use the Dosciere Store.

That same spring when our first chicks hatched, Josephine quickly claimed a little yellow chick. She fed and petted it every day, and it became so gentle she could pick it up anytime in the yard. As it turned out, the chick was a pullet instead of a rooster. As Josephine petted and fed it, it would sing like the yard hens did when they were hunting a nest for laying. The song went, "Quooonk, quooonk," so that was what Josephine named her. She would say, "Sing, and I will give you some corn," and the hen would sing each time she was asked. We kept Quonk-Quonk for many years, and she gave us lots of eggs. We kept petting and feeding her, and she sang for any of us. One day she was missing, and we assume a hawk caught her.

Lucy's first calf was born that spring on a Friday in May, so we named her Friday May. She did not become a kicker because Mama petted her daily, every time she got a chance, so Friday May was very gentle.

That year Grandpa Judy was living in that little house he had built on Mr. Shipp's place not far from where we lived. I do remember that sometimes Josephine and I spent a few days with him during the summertime. Grandpa was not a well-educated man because he was born at the end of the War between the States. Even when he reached school age, all the schools in South Carolina, where he lived then, were still in chaos, as were most of the southern states. This was because of the poorly-organized government and the northern carpetbaggers who had come to our part of the country. Most of these men were dishonest and really cared little about re-establishing the South. They were selfish and were only interested in what they could get for themselves.

My grandpa was, however, a smart man and very quick to learn. Somehow he had learned to read printing, such as a newspaper, but the only writing he could do was to sign his name. He had a lot of ingenuity when it came to his woodwork. He liked to work with wood and made a number of useful items for himself and others. This was one of the ways he supported himself. He devised ways to use hand tools to make things that most people made with machinery. For instance, he devised a lathe, which he worked with one foot while standing on the other. That year he made small rocking chairs for Josephine and me. These chairs were in our family for over twenty-three years.

He made both straight and rocking chairs from hickory and ash. He made bread trays from tupelo-gum wood, which was almost as lightweight as cork and nearly snow-white when dried. People really did like all his work. Income from this trade supplemented his farming. He learned to use a steel square and became a good carpenter. He also grew his own tobacco and made his own corn-cob pipe. He was a frugal man who lived a simple life. He always wore denim overalls and a denim jacket. He only wore a shirt under his jacket when it was cold weather. In summer he always wore a straw hat; in winter, a dark felt hat. Almost all the time he had a mustache. One summer he shaved off his mustache and bought a different hat. He passed by our house on the road, and even my mama did not recognize him.

Daddy told me that he had seen Grandpa take off his boots, have someone place them on his back with his folded overalls and jumper on the boots, put his hat on his head, and swim the Boeuf River with a smoking pipe in his mouth. None of the clothes got wet. This was amazing to Daddy because Daddy could not swim at all. Grandpa liked to hunt and fish. The young men of the area enjoyed going possum hunting and coon hunting with him. Grandpa loved to eat the game meat from his hunting trips.

I remember quite a few things about the summer of 1932. We lived in Caldwell Parish but near the Richland

Parish line. When there was a revival at Amity Church in Richland Parish, a friend who had an open wagon pulled with a team came by to take us to church. Mama and Daddy knew people in both communities, so everyone was happy to see one another again. All the children sat in the wagon bed on a quilt while the grownups sat on seats up front. The older children were allowed to sit on the very back of the wagon and dangle their feet off the end, but I was too young to do that. That was an exciting experience for us children.

When school started in the fall, we did not have to cross the river any longer. We walked a couple of miles to the Girod School. This was a larger school with more grades and more students. We attended there for only three months because the cold winter weather prevented us from regular attendance in December.

That winter of 1932–33, we had an awful cold spell of rain, sleet, and snow. The freezing rain formed long icicles on the roof. The low places froze over, and the hogs that were out in open range did not come home to be fed. Daddy put nails in the soles of some old shoes to prevent him from slipping on the ice and went back into the woods carrying a sack of corn on his back. He found the hogs and fed them some to keep them from starving. As soon as the freeze was over, the hogs came up to the house, and Daddy penned them up and fed them.

I remember that Lucy and Friday May were standing out in the cold weather. We had a little corn crib but no shelter for the cows. We felt so sorry for them. Mama took our cotton sacks, ripped them open on one side, and put them over the cows, tying them under their necks. The rain came down and froze and made a sheet of ice on those sacks, but the cows lived through that really cold spell.

FRUGAL FARM LIFE

Our family didn't have very much and had to learn how to raise most of what we ate. We had milk and butter most of the year. During the months that a milk cow was dried up, we would not have milk, but once her calf was born, we could begin milking again. The calf was given all it needed, and soon we had plenty of milk. We always tried to have a garden.

Whenever we could we canned vegetables, but it was hard at that time to can anything except what we could can by open-kettle method. That method was a simple way to can and required only filling the sanitized jars and sealing them. We would can tomatoes like that, but today's recommendation is to use the "water bath" method, which is to submerge the filled jars in boiling water for various lengths of time, depending on the food. Open-kettle method was used at that time extensively for the sweets and foods with acid. We never knew of a jar of tomatoes that we had canned to spoil. If we canned things like string beans or okra, they required a water bath for about three hours. It was summertime, and it took a lot of stove wood to keep that water boiling that long. This made the kitchen hot and made the process expensive in time and stove wood thus making it more difficult to can peas, okra, and corn that did not have acid like tomatoes. We canned fruit like apples, peaches, and berries that had plenty of acid in them. We didn't have to can with sugar but had to have it when we opened the fruit to sweeten it enough to eat. A pressure cooker would certainly have simplified canning, but we did not have one.

In the summertime Mama usually didn't cook a hot supper, but we ate leftover cornbread, peas, and maybe corn. We had plenty of corn and often ate it fried, which was a method of cooking field corn in an iron skillet with some pork lard and a small amount of sugar to help it brown a little. The top of the kernels were thinly cut off and discarded, then the corn was scraped from the cob and put into the skillet. It had to be stirred frequently to keep it from burning, but the brown bits gave flavor. When it became thick, Mama added water in the skillet and put a lid on it for simmering but still stirred it occasionally. It was similar to today's cream corn, only much better. Everyone liked Mama's fried corn.

We ate chickens in the summer and lots of okra, both boiled and fried. Fried okra was cooked in an iron skillet with lard and salt, stirred frequently, and allowed to brown a little. It was then steamed with a lid on the skillet for a while, so it was really smothered okra. It was easy to grow and was good for us. In the winter we usually had plenty of pork, either smoked bacon, ham, or sausage, to eat with our dried peas, tomato gravy, and cornbread. We had beef only when Mama occasionally bought a beef soup bone in the wintertime. It usually had some meat and fat, and she really enjoyed beef soup with tomatoes and macaroni. Possibly this is where she got the tallow she saved for our tallow rags, which were used on our chests for colds in the winter.

When we girls came down with a cold, Mama's first thought was to put a tallow rag on our chest. It was sometimes made of old flannel cloth. She would coat it well on one side with tallow, which is beef fat, then she would add sprinkles of turpentine, camphor, and Vick's salve. The tallow helped prevent irritation to our skin. As simple as this might sound, it certainly seemed to help. I don't know why turpentine was used, but it was only a small amount. Many times in those days people had to use simple home remedies because they could not easily get to a doctor.

Mama made tomato gravy in winter from canned tomatoes and in summer from fresh peeled and sliced tomatoes, starting with a light brown roux. She added salt and a little pepper and sometimes a pinch of sugar to cut the tartness then let this simmer and thicken. Sometimes for a change she added onions. It was delicious on cornbread or biscuits, so we probably had it for breakfast some mornings. We seldom used much pepper because that was one of those things that had to be purchased and could be omitted. It was more expensive during World War II because it was imported. We used both black and red pepper and sage when making sausage. We sometimes grew our own sage and red pepper. The red peppers were first dried then lightly roasted and ground in a sausage mill fitted with a pepper plate, which ground it very fine.

Mama often planted tomato seeds in a tub on the back porch in early spring and then transplanted them into the garden after warmer weather. This was very smart on her part, as it gave the tomato plants an early start. She taught me gardening, canning, how to take care of the produce, and as much as she could about cooking. What I did not learn from her, I later learned in school. I still enjoy cooking today.

Hog killing was an exciting time. It meant fresh pork, which we had not had for several months. I did not like the idea of killing the hog that we had been feeding in a floored pen for months, but it was necessary. We killed only one large hog each winter. Daddy fed it only water and shelled corn for a good while before it was killed. After it was dead, Daddy quickly pierced its throat with a knife to rid the body of excess blood. Then it was put head first into very hot water in a barrel that was secured at an angle in the ground.

Daddy in 1940 with hog he killed.

The hog would be so large that only half of its body would fit into the barrel at a time. After a couple of minutes the hog was flipped over and tested to see if the hair was slipping enough to be pulled out. When the hair came out easily, the hog was pulled out and then put back in so that its hind parts were in the scalding water. The hair was tested once again, and the hog was flipped so that both sides were ready for the hair to be pulled out. The hog was then pulled out of the barrel onto the grass, and the hair was removed from the entire hog. This chore was done as quickly as possible before the hair on the hog cooled.

The entire hog was then rinsed and hung from a limb on a tree and washed thoroughly a second time. No matter what color the hog had been, it was now snow-white. The cavity was emptied and washed inside, and then the meat was ready to be cut up for the salting and curing process.

We enjoyed some of the pork fresh, like liver and spare ribs. It was cold weather, and of course our entire kitchen was like an ice box, so the fresh pork could be safely kept for several days. We usually made some sausage and, of course, cracklings. To make the cracklings, we ground the excess fat with a course blade in the sausage mill, making sure there was no skin included. This was cooked until brown and no moisture remained. The fat was then strained into buckets and sealed while still hot. This fat was what we used for cooking everything, and it kept well into the spring. The cracklings that had been strained out were delicious with baked potatoes and other foods.

It seems we ate a lot of pork and bread because that is what we had, but we all worked hard on the farm. This hard work was probably what helped keep us healthy. We did not have as much fresh fruit as we would have liked, so it was a real treat when we did get some at Christmastime. We really enjoyed receiving bananas, oranges, shiny red apples, and Brazil nuts for the holidays. On special occasions, like a birthday or for company or sometimes on a weekend, Mama would open a jar of fruit, add sugar, and make a cobbler. She didn't know how to make a pie crust, so she used extra biscuits for the bottom and in the middle of the cobbler. We usually had fresh cream for the top. That was definitely good eating!

Sometimes we made chow chow. It was our main relish and was made of cabbage, cucumbers, green tomatoes, peppers, onion, vinegar, and spices. All the ingredients were ground in the food chopper and cooked in a large enamel dishpan with enough sugar to temper the sour taste. It was put in quart jars and sealed. It was not necessary to use the water bath. During the war times, our sugar was rationed so we would be careful to make it go as far as possible. Sometimes we used prepared mustard in a relish. The relish made the peas and cornbread taste very good.

We ordered most items needed, including material, from Sears, Roebuck and Co. What a friend this company was to us and other farm people who could not go to town very often! The catalog usually came in late summer or early fall, and we used it frequently. We always looked forward to the new catalog each year. Shipping was very reasonable—charged by weight—so a small package of material and trimmings might total only two or three dollars. We never considered ordering a readymade dress because of the expense and the chance of poor workmanship. We were a poor family, but we appreciated well-made clothes. Therefore, sometimes people thought we were better off than we were because of our well-made clothes.

I began to learn to sew at the age of ten, making some dresses for my sister Margie, who was born that spring of 1936. I also made a dress for myself that summer and continue to make many of my own clothes to this day at age eighty-one, not to mention most all of my older daughter's clothes. Linda does not sew but is typing this book for me. My younger daughter Judy learned to sew quite well and has done sewing for herself and family as time permitted. My sisters Margie and Sue are also good seamstresses and have made clothes for themselves and family.

Daddy had a suit that he had purchased in better times that Mama would brush and press. He wore it to church sometimes, but in the summertime it was not uncommon for men to go in shirtsleeves because it was so hot. I know there were no electric fans in the church, but we did have cardboard fans, which were often given away by insurance companies, funeral homes, and other businesses. Sometimes they were kept in the church pews because they were *freebies*. The ladies and some older men used these at church. Some people had fans made of palmetto blades that were oval in shape and bound around the edge. Those were more substantial but belonged to individuals.

This frugal way of life was common among the country people, but people who owned their own land did not have to move every year like we did. Mama never complained about her life because Daddy was doing the best he could. Mama was a hard worker, and she loved Jesus. She taught us to work hard as well. She loved music and often sang hymns around the house as she worked. She did the best she could to raise her children and provide for them even though she and Daddy were poor. Her mother had died when she was only four years old. Mama became a mother like she would have liked to have had and was a wonderful mother to us girls.

A Family Loss

After that terribly cold December of 1932, between Christmas and the New Year, we moved back across the river into Richland Parish again. I was in the second grade, and Josephine was in third grade. She was a year or two behind because she did not get to start first grade as early as she should have due to the fact that we had moved a lot in Mississippi. In January 1933 we started to school at Woolen Lake School, walking at least a mile or more. When we came home that first day, she said she did not feel well, so we didn't go to school the next day. Josephine stayed in bed, but I don't remember what her complaints were, as I was only six and one-half years old. It was a very cold January, and Mama used quart jars of hot water around Josephine to keep her warm. Daddy sent word by someone going to Columbia that a doctor was needed. Dr. Adams came out to our house.

He said she had a leakage of the heart, which was due to a dysfunctional valve, along with pleurisy and Bright's disease, all of which were very serious. It was especially serious during that time, as we did not have sulfa drugs, penicillin, or antibiotics. She died on January 13, 1933. Mama cried quietly as she continued her daily chores. Daddy was visibly upset. I was certainly distraught, not only from the loss of my sister, but from the suffering of my parents.

Some neighbors built a casket for her and lined it inside and out with white cloth. Mr. Sanford Etier was our landlord that year. His wife, Audrey, made Josephine a dress out of blue broadcloth. It had long sleeves and a belt. She had white stockings on her feet. They put boards across from one bed to another to lay her out on as a cooling board and then later put her into the casket. The casket was put into another box made of unpainted lumber and put in a boat to be paddled across the Boeuf River. We all went across the river in boats, as it was a long way to go around to a bridge, and few people had cars at that time. It was not very far across the river by boat. She was buried in Duchesne Cemetery across the river in Caldwell Parish. When we came back home, we were all terribly sad.

We had just moved to this new place, and I did not yet know anyone in the community except the landlord's children, Annie Mae and Buddy Etier. Sometimes we walked to school together. It seems to me now that I must have been in a dazed state after losing Josephine because I was alone and had no playmate at home. I missed her company all the time. It was very depressing for Mama, Daddy, and me.

I went back to school at Woolen Lake School. Of course, I had to walk to school alone a lot of the time, but sometimes there were other children in the community who walked with me. School was in a two-room building with a wide hall between the two large rooms. Mrs. Ethel Murray was the teacher. Later that year one side of the building was used for church services. Mr. H.K. Lineback, who was a church planter from Arkansas, came to our community to start a church in the spring of 1933. He asked the local people what denomination of church they wanted. Mr. Lineback was Presbyterian, but most of the people in our area wanted a Baptist church, and so it was.

Mama and I went to church there, and Daddy went some too. He could not always go with us, but he loved the singing at church. He had attended country singing schools as a young man in Mississippi. He knew shaped notes and timing and had a good bass voice. Mama was elected as the teacher for the card class, which included the early primary children, probably from first to third grade. I don't know how many different classes we had for Sunday school, but our class was out in the hall. We didn't have chairs, so we stood. Mama would give the children the cards every week to take home to learn the memory verse. When we came back to Sunday school the next Sunday, we were supposed to answer roll with a Bible verse. Some children did and some didn't. We were all supposed to memorize the memory verse, and then she would read the Bible story on the card and explain it to us.

After Sunday school we would go in the side of the building where the adults were meeting and have singing and preaching. I can't remember if we had a preacher every Sunday or who it was all the time, but I know there was a preacher named Reverend Lavell Calhoun who walked from Columbia. This was a long walk unless he was given a ride part of the way. Usually his family was not with him as they attended their regular church, and he was like a missionary for us. On special occasions they came to our church with him. Many years later, for a short time, I roomed with Brother Calhoun's youngest daughter, Lurlean, in Minden, Louisiana, when we both worked there.

A nice memory from that summer of 1933 is the swing Daddy built for me beside our house. I loved swinging in that swing, but it made me very nauseated every time. Then I would get over it and swing again later in the day or the next day and get sick again. Finally I got used to swinging enough that it didn't make me sick. My friend Lucille Wheeler, who lived about a mile through the woods, would come over to play. She could swing longer and higher than I, and she never got sick. During that summer Lucille was running and stumped her toe, and her head struck a root. She was hurt badly from this head injury and died shortly afterward. I missed her so much because she was my only playmate.

That was the summer the government required all the cotton farmers to plow up some of their cotton crop. Each farmer had to plow up a percentage of his cotton for which he was paid a small sum. We didn't understand it fully then, and Daddy was very distraught because he had a very good crop that year. Probably every farmer had a good crop, and the government expected a surplus of cotton, which would have meant lower prices for everyone. Not long afterward we noticed the price of all cotton goods went up, especially yard goods for clothing. What we once paid ten cents per yard for went up to twelve cents then later to fifteen cents per yard. As the years went by, the price of material gradually went down to ten cents a yard.

In the fall of 1933, I started to school again at Woolen Lake School in the third grade. Two more tragic things happened in 1933. That winter a large family in the community came down with pneumonia and was all sick at one time. The neighbors took turns sitting with them day and night. Daddy took several turns at night until the family recovered. Several family members were sick so long that even after recovery they had to learn to walk again. Another lady in the community who had a mental illness doused herself with gasoline and set herself on fire. The fire was smothered out, but she was horribly burned and lived only several days.

We moved again that winter of 1933 just before Christmas, this time closer to Columbia across the Ouachita River from Corey. We lived on the bluff side very close to the bank of the river. At this point my Grandpa Judy, who was about seventy years old by then, came to live with us. In order to get our cows to the new place, Grandpa and Daddy led Lucy, our main milk cow, down the road, and Friday May and a couple of yearlings followed. When the yearlings sometimes ran off the road, Daddy had to chase them. This move was especially hard for men and cows. When Daddy got the cows to the new place, he turned them out on the free range and then came back for me and Mama and our household items. We had to cross two rivers, the Boeuf and Ouachita rivers, with our household belongings on a flatboat, or barge.

For Christmas that year, Daddy purchased the usual small amount of fruit and Brazil nuts and one toy for me. It was a small stuffed dog about eight inches tall, and when I patted him on his head, he yelped. Times really were hard.

The new place in 1934 was near the hill country but in the flat area. During the early winter months, we had no hay for our cows, so the Spanish moss was their main feed source. There the old oak trees were loaded with Spanish moss. Daddy and Grandpa would cut down the moss-laden trees, and when the cows heard them chopping or sawing, they came running. The cows just loved the Spanish moss. I asked Mama why they liked it so much, and she said it probably tasted good. I put some in my mouth and chewed it a little bit. It had a sweet taste, but I spat it out. Later the trees were cut up for firewood for our cookstove and fireplace.

To get to town for shopping in Columbia, Daddy had to cross the Ouachita River at Corey and usually catch a ride with someone. The main boat landing was near the house of our landlord Fred Winn. Several other families lived nearby. People in that time gladly offered rides and were not afraid to do so, as most folks knew one another. This was how Daddy bought the few groceries that we had to buy.

Joseph Clarence Laird, 1934

Walking to school at the age of seven was not very easy for me. I had to go about a quarter of a mile through our field down a turn-row to the gate. Then there was a stretch of woods to walk through to get to the next field, but there were cows in the woods. This was scary to me as a small child, and I watched those cows carefully each morning and afternoon. They never bothered me, but that did not keep me from the fear that they might. When I got to the next field and closed the gate behind me to keep the cows from getting in the field, it was another quarter mile to the neighbor's house where Mr. D.C. McLain's children joined me for the rest of the walk to the bus stop. Muddy weather made this journey more difficult because the bus could not always get up one of the steeper hills in this area. We had to walk farther on muddy days.

This year I attended Ward 5 School in the community near Kemp's store. This school was larger than any I had attended before and went through high school—eleven grades. I was in the third grade, and my teacher was Miss Cecil Carr. She was a good teacher, and I liked her. That year I missed a lot of days because Mama and Daddy pulled me out of school during the time so many children had the measles. So much of the time back then pneumonia followed measles and was fatal to many children.

I always took a lunch to school and some years had a rectangular metal lunch box with a handle. Biscuit sandwiches were made each morning from a variety of foods. Sometimes I had ham or sausage, and sometimes it was egg salad. If I had fresh milk still warm from the cow, I would always put it in my pocket to keep one hand warm. Mama would have put it in a bottle, possibly a former vanilla extract bottle. In the winter we sat at our desks for lunch, but we went outside in warm weather.

There was a boat crossing near our house, and the boat was always left on our side of the river, but it did not belong to us. So when we heard voices from across the river calling for the boat, many times Mama was the one who took the boat across to get the people, and they would paddle back. She could not swim, so this was rather dangerous, especially when the river was high and the wind was blowing up big waves. Daddy was in the fields much of the time, so Mama felt it was her responsibility to help.

That summer when I was eight years old, I often stood on the bank of the river. I loved seeing the steam boats going by to Columbia and then coming back. These were cargo boats, but if the pilot waved, I loved waving back. I feel sure they carried cotton and feed and other cargo to other ports.

Sometimes I would walk about two hundred yards down the turn-row where Daddy was pumping water at noon for his mule. Then I would get to ride back to the house on the mule when Daddy came in for his dinner. This was the only time I was permitted to ride the mule, and it was a lot of fun. Work animals were not for our recreation.

Lillian riding mule, age 8

That summer I watched Mama make a quilt as a wedding gift for the daughter of her best friend. The top and bottom of the quilt were made from flour sacks that Mama dyed in pink and yellow squares. I became so interested that I began piecing my first quilt. The top was made in a nine-patch pattern from scraps from our dresses. I was piecing it by hand and having difficulty because my needle was too long for my fingers. It was many years later that I finished that quilt top; Mama finally allowed me to finish it on the sewing machine. Mama did not make many quilts at that time of her life because she was so busy with field and housework. It was not until as a widow when she was living with me that she and I together pieced and quilted numerous quilts for ourselves and family members.

This was about the time that President Roosevelt's administration started the commodity program. Commodities were given to many poor families as food supplements. The only food I remember getting that year was oatmeal, but I am sure there were others. This was a new food to me, but I liked it. We had plenty of milk or cream with sugar to put on it.

That same year Lucy had another heifer calf, which we named Augustine because she was born in August. She turned out to be a good milk cow but had a wild streak like her mama, Lucy. We had Augustine for many years, and she gave us calves every year. Friday May had her first calf that year.

Grandpa Judy was almost seventy years old by this time. It was in the summertime that he became ill with a high fever and *night sweats,* which left him weak. Grandpa stayed in bed many days that summer because we had no way to get him to a doctor. Mama knew that he had been ill in this same manner once before when he lived in South Carolina. She wrote to the doctor there who had treated him before. In answer to her letter, we received a package with a bottle of medicine and instructions. Mama's inquiry was answered by the grandson of the doctor she had written. Grandpa took the medicine and quickly began to improve. I don't know what the medicine was, but we were all very thankful to see him well again. Grandpa was very helpful with the outdoor chores. He was able to return to his activities of helping with the gardening and taking care of our chickens, hogs, and cows.

It was at this farm that summer of 1934 that Mama took a picture of me with the sow nursing her pigs. That sow had been the little pig that Mama had rescued from her wild mother four years previously.

In the fall I returned to school at Ward 5 in the third grade again, because I had failed due to being held out while others had the measles. Mama and Daddy picked cotton that fall, but when it came to getting it to the gin, it had to be done differently. Because we could not load a wagon with loose cotton to cross the river, it had to be packed very tightly and stuffed into burlap bags. Then the bags were sewn with hemp string and tied at the top then loaded into the wagon to take to the ferry. There they were transferred across the river and reloaded to a truck for the six-mile trip to Columbia.

When Daddy became dissatisfied with our situation for whatever reason (poor land, inconvenient location, etc.), he would begin seeking out a better situation for us. Sometimes he would hear from a neighbor or from someone in town of a landowner who needed help. Daddy was quite a talker and made friends easily. Whenever he was in Columbia he would gather with other farmers and talk. This is probably how he knew about new possibilities.

That December found us moving once again. Just before Christmas we moved closer to the Ward 5 School. The move did not require us crossing a river this time. The school bus actually picked me up in front of the house. Our new landlord, Mr. Bill Ray, moved us in his truck. Somehow he managed to get the truck in from the hillside to our house. The new house was larger than any we had before. It had a large front porch, a large front room with a fireplace, three small bedrooms, a dining room, and a kitchen with a pantry. The water source was a dug well with a roof over it. We had always had a pump before this time. I had never seen a well like that before but learned to use the pulley to draw water. I was very excited about this new house because I had my own bedroom for the first time.

The fireplace had a stick-and-dirt chimney. Most chimneys were made of brick, so this was unusual for this period of time. When we noticed repairs were needed, Grandpa Judy knew how to repair the chimney and made the necessary repairs so the fireplace was safe. As usual the outhouse was in the backyard. We had a barn, a smokehouse, and a large garden area. Grandpa Judy made this move with us. We had a large garden that year. We also had beehives, which gave us honey. Our mailman was Mr. J.C. Wilkins, whose son James became a good friend to my husband many years later in Columbia.

We raised chickens, ducks, and geese at this place. We turned the ducks and geese into the cotton field where the ducks ate worms and bowl weevils, and the geese ate the grass. There was a creek nearby, so Grandpa Judy and I fished there a few times. He found an especially deep hole where he often caught pike. Pike are not very large and have tiny scales and no bones except back and rib bones. We all enjoyed eating the pike.

There was a shallow pond in the pasture with a mayhaw tree in the center. In late spring Daddy would wade out into the pond and shake that tree so the mayhaws would fall and float. He scooped them up, and we made mayhaw butter. We sweetened it and canned some. Mayhaws are a fruit about the size of a small plum. They are red on the outside, much like an apple, and about the color of an apple inside. They grow in low, damp places. Daddy loved cakes stacked with mayhaw butter because it made the cakes very moist. Mayhaws also make good jelly.

We also had fruit trees out front, so we canned peaches and apples that summer. I had turned nine years old in June, and Mama said I could use a sharp knife to peel the tomatoes and fruit. Our garden gave us greens in the spring and fall. We also had tomatoes, okra, green onions, cucumbers, squash, butter beans, and snap beans. Grandpa liked all these fresh vegetables, but his favorite foods were wild game, especially possum. He killed and dressed them, and Mama cooked them. She liked game meat also, but Daddy did not.

While living at the Ray place, we attended church at Fellowship Baptist Church. The building had been at one time a schoolhouse where our neighbor Johnny Kelly had taught. The road to the church was a dirt road with no gravel. People in the community laid small tree trunks very closely across part of the road to prevent cars from getting stuck in the mud. This was called a corduroy road.

Mr. Clayton Haddox was my teacher in the fourth grade class that fall at Ward 5 School. I enjoyed Mr. Haddox as a teacher and especially enjoyed the songs we learned that year. We did not have a piano but sang many of Stephen Foster's songs. Many years later I met Mr. Haddox again at a P.T.A. meeting at the junior high school in Bastrop where my daughters attended school for two years.

DEATH OF GOVERNOR HUEY P. LONG

That fall our cotton crop was slim indeed. Before ours was ready, Mr. Wesley Carr had cotton ready to pick. Mama and Daddy decided they would go pick cotton for Mr. Carr to earn a little extra money until ours was ready. I stayed at the Carr home one day to play with Merl, who was a girl about my age. It was during the day when the family was listening to the radio that we all heard of the tragic news of the death of Governor Huey P. Long. He had been shot down in the capitol in Baton Rouge. We did not have a radio at home at that time, so we would not have heard this news for a while except by this coincidence of circumstances.

Times in our country were extremely hard during the winter of 1935. President Franklin Roosevelt ordered the people who had starving cattle and no way to feed them to have them slaughtered. Folks were given a small amount for slaughtering their cattle, and that way there was less cattle and more feed. I didn't understand this at the time. Daddy felt he had to slaughter Lucy because she was older, harder to milk, and was not withstanding the winter weather well, but he kept Friday May and Augustine.

Mr. Bill Ray's land that we worked in 1935 was not very productive. It was hill land, sandy and not good for a cotton crop like the rich soil near the Boeuf River. If memory serves me, Daddy made only two bales of cotton, five hundred pounds each, at three cents per pound. That was thirty dollars profit for a year's work, which was so little that he felt he had to move again. There seemed to always be something wrong with the situation, and this time it was the land

Mr. and Mrs. Ray were very nice people and had been good landlords. They had helped us move to this farm, but now it was time to move on. Before we moved we celebrated Christmas at this house. Mama and Daddy had promised me rubber boots for Christmas. So when it snowed a few days before Christmas, I begged them to let me have my boots early, which they did. I had made a Christmas tree from the top of a young sweet gum tree. Mama let me dust it with flour so it looked like snow. Decorations on the tree consisted of tinfoil-wrapped sweet gum balls. When Christmas came I got a lovely cardboard nativity scene that was to be punched out, folded, and set up. Best of all, I got the rubber baby doll from the Sears catalog that I had selected. It cost fifty-nine cents. Mama had made it a blue figured dress and bonnet with lace. She even made a slip with lace trim. It was a good Christmas for me. I still have that doll dress and slip.

In January 1936 we moved to the Riverton community. Grandpa Judy did not move with us this time. He stayed with his good friends and neighbors Johnny and Mattie Kelly. Our landlady's name was Miss Helen Vaughter, who owned land about five miles north of Columbia near the Ouachita River. This was still Caldwell Parish. Daddy had agreed to work by the day, probably for one dollar per day. But when there were days that Miss Vaughter had no work for him, he realized he needed to renegotiate the agreement. She agreed for him to raise a crop on part of the land.

The school at Riverton was a medium-sized school with first through sixth grades. It was close to the overpass on the road to Monroe. I had to walk quite a ways to school, possibly two miles. There were several children walking along there, and we sometimes walked along the railroad tracks. Other times we walked around the road that followed the river. There were some older homes on this road, one of which was a large plantation-type home. It was a fine house with a veranda that reached the breadth of the house. The Hill family lived there, and sometimes we children would stop in warm weather and talk to the parrot that would be outside in his cage on the veranda. When we said, "Goodbye, Polly," and left, it would say, "Come back again."

I don't remember much about the school except that I did not enjoy school much that year because I was behind due to having moved so much and missed so much school. Miss Thelma Fisher was my teacher that spring in the fourth grade, and I ended up repeating it that fall with her as my teacher again.

That year Daddy planted cotton on halves. Miss Helen would get half of the money when it was sold. Things didn't cost as much then, but we didn't have much money to spend. In 1936 I can remember that we could buy cotton material for dresses for about ten cents per yard, but dimes were hard to come by during the Depression years. Our clothes were all homemade, but Daddy worked in chambray shirts and denim overalls, which had to be bought.

Spring brought a new little sister to our house. Margie Faye Louise was born March 2, 1936. Daddy planted the cotton that spring, and because Margie was so little and still nursing, Mama did not chop cotton that year. Daddy and I had that chore to ourselves. Chopping thinned the crop, leaving about three stalks per hill, about eight inches apart. I was only ten that summer and not near as fast at chopping as Daddy, but I could chop fifty feet to his one hundred feet. This was a big help to him, and I felt like I was almost grown to get this responsibility.

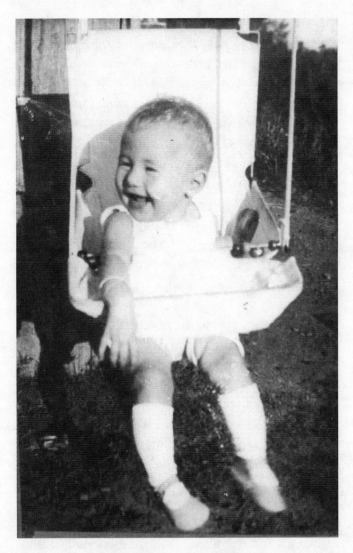

Margie Faye, 6 months old, 1936

We chopped the cotton until every row had been thinned. Naturally, the more rows of cotton, the longer this chore took. If there was a lot of grass in the cotton after chopping was finished, then we sometimes went back and hoed the grass out wherever needed. We didn't need to hoe much that year because we had brought our geese from the previous place. When the cotton was up only a few inches, it was time to take the geese into the cotton field to eat the grass. They did not eat weeds or any of the cotton. I was "goose girl" and had the responsibility six days a week of driving them slowly through the field, waving a flag on the end of a fishing pole. They did not trample the cotton but moved slowly through the field, feeding on grass as they went. I wore a large brimmed straw hat because it was summertime and hot. This was an all-day job until cotton-chopping time came. At noon and before day's end, I took the geese to the nearby ditch for water.

That summer at the age of ten, I became very interested in sewing, so Mama taught me what she knew. We didn't have patterns, but Mama did all the cutting by another dress or garment. I sometimes do this myself today. I learned to use the treadle sewing machine and to make buttonholes by hand. As I learned more in school, I began to make my own clothes, which allowed me to have more for less money.

I continued to sew throughout my high school years and have for many years sewn for my children and family and neighbors. Some of these skills learned early have served me well all my life. After I married and had children of my own, I did not live on a farm;

but the sewing and cooking skills came in handy, and I have had a garden in many places where we lived.

Lillian, age 10; Margie, age 5 mo., 1936)

We did not have a garden that year for several reasons; however, we had moved our beehives there from the Ray place. We didn't enjoy honey as much as the cane syrup but were glad to have it after all our syrup was used up. We raised hogs and still had some milk cows. We did not have a well at the house, so I had to go to the artesian well near Miss Helen's house to get drinking water. The coldest water came from the main well, which was in Miss Helen's garden. There near the well was a row of red onions almost as big as baseballs bulging out of the ground. They looked so delicious. Before I knew it I stooped and pulled one up. When I got home with the cold water and the red onion, I had to explain what I had done. I knew what I had done was wrong but did not feel very guilty until Mama and Daddy scolded me soundly and sent me back to Miss Helen's to return the onion with a dime to give her. She was at work in Monroe, but her mother graciously accepted the onion and the dime, realizing it was a lesson for me. And it was a good lesson.

A very nice memory from 1936 was the time Mrs. Vaughter invited me to go with her to Monroe to see a movie. I had never before seen one, of course, and the movie starred Shirley Temple in *Poor Little Rich Girl*. I was very excited at this outing and enjoyed it very much. I had seen a picture of Shirley Temple in the Sears catalog advertising their material. I chose that particular piece of material, and Mama made me a dress just like it but only longer. Seeing her in the movie made the little girl in the catalog come alive. I found the story to be very sad and assumed it was a true story of her life. I found out later, of course, that it was not. On the way home that day we stopped for ice cream. We had banana nut ice cream in a double cone. It was the best I ever had.

Another outing that year was with Mrs. Vaughter and her daughter Miss Helen, who attended a very large Episcopal church in Monroe. It had kneeling benches and was very different from any church I had ever attended. Every lady was required to wear a hat, so I wore one of Miss Helen's sister's white tams. Miss Helen played a violin solo that Sunday. While in Monroe that day, we drove by Mrs. Vaughter's church, which was a large Presbyterian church. These were beautiful churches and in such contrast to the country churches I had attended.

A FINAL MOVE

In December 1936 we moved to Mr. Richard Hatch's place in Richland Parish near Buckner Store. My parents had lived there in 1922. It was just before Christmas, but we did not have much of a celebration that year.

The previous year had been hard, and we had not had a garden that year. We did not move the beehives, but the new place had several seedling peach trees and a garden spot where there were clumps of winter onions growing. The onions were flat sided because they grew close together. Mama was glad to have these because we did not have onion sets to put out that year. We didn't have the knowledge or equipment to spray the peach trees, so there were not many good peaches when they were ripe in the summer. We cut off the good part of each peach and canned them without sugar.

The first year at the Hatch place, Daddy planned the fields. He walked over the land, taking note of the soil and drainage of the fields. In this way he was able to decide what crop to plant in each area. He planted cotton and corn in the spring, which were our main crops. Then he planted peas of different kinds about three weeks apart. He liked whippoorwills, black-eyed peas, crowders, and purple hulls. These peas all tasted different and ripened at different times. We ate peas freely when they were green and saved them after they dried for winter food. We did not have to share the peas with the landlord because this was for our personal food source. However, we always took a fresh mess of peas to them whenever each type was ripe. This was the neighborly thing to do, and they always appreciated it. Peas were one of our main food sources.

We had a nice garden that year, and we began canning tomatoes and peaches. The peaches were not the best, but they made good pies. We had to add sugar to them when we opened them. Daddy was pleased with his arrangement with Mr. Richard Hatch and his wife, Mrs. Flossie Hatch. Whenever we had fresh corn or peas, we shared with them. The tools and mules were kept in the big barn, so Daddy went up to their house often and took them some fresh vegetables from the garden. There was no restriction on how many peas and food sources we could plant for our personal use.

We almost always had a row of watermelons and cantaloupes, and that year was no exception. Daddy always used natural fertilizer, as he thought that made better melons. We didn't always have ripe melons by July 4, but we had them soon after. Not having an icebox, we gathered the ripe melons and put them under the bed so they would stay cool. We all enjoyed the watermelons. Mama occasionally made watermelon rind preserves when she had enough sugar on hand. She sometimes pickled tiny watermelons that came on the vines so late they had no chance of maturing. She made them into crispy pickles, sometimes with pepper to make them spicy. We enjoyed fresh cantaloupes, but one of Daddy's favorite preserves was made from very ripe cantaloupes, or musk melons.

It was at this farm place that we had so much milk and butter in the spring that we could not use it all. Daddy bargained with a neighbor who had a large family of children to do some work for him in exchange for skim milk and butter. The neighbor agreed to cut and dig up the thorn bushes out of our field, because the mules would not plow close to them. This was hard work and took many days, but the man was very glad to have the work and receive milk and butter for his family. Daddy was happy to have someone else do that hard work so he could spend his time plowing and getting ready to plant the crop.

Our family was Baptist, but the only church nearby was a Pentecostal church, which was about a mile and a half from our house. Naturally, we had to walk there. I had not been saved at that time, but we all enjoyed going to church, and Daddy especially enjoyed the singing. We went as often as we could, but it was cold in the winter and hot in the summer. In the summertime the fieldwork took most of our time and effort.

Services were not held every Sunday, and there was

no regular pastor. Preachers from other communities would come at various times. The building was made of rough unpainted lumber, as were the benches. The floor was sawdust. The only lights were kerosene or Coleman lanterns. Services were usually at night. I do remember an Easter service one year in the morning and an egg hunt and dinner on the ground afterward.

I started back to school in the fall, repeating the fourth grade at age ten in a one-room schoolhouse called Union School. It was next door to the Union Methodist Church and had grades one through five. There were only two of us in the fourth grade, and the other student was Myrtis Froust. Our teacher was Mrs. Mhoon Hatch, who was married to Mr. Mac Hatch, a brother to Richard Hatch, our landlord. We walked out to the gravel road to meet her and rode with her to the school. Sometimes I would be late getting to the meeting point, and she would have to go on to school without me. I would then walk the whole way, which was about three more miles.

It would be recess time before I got to school on those days, but I didn't miss class because Mrs. Mhoon would have started classes first with the younger children. Fourth grade began right after recess. When the fourth graders were called up front to the recitation bench, Myrtis and I would take turns answering questions. We studied geography that year, and I really enjoyed learning about the states and other countries. It was interesting to learn what crops and goods were made in other countries and what goods were produced, manufactured, and exported.

There were no fifth graders that year in the school. It was at the recitation bench that we discussed the lesson, answered questions, and then returned to our desks. Our teacher often gave us study sheets with many questions covering the lesson, and we studied them carefully prior to test day. She reviewed the study sheets with us before the tests and then used many of the same questions for test day. I learned a lot that year from Mrs. Mhoon Hatch.

That summer I had many chores to do. My morning chores included making the beds, sweeping the floors, washing the dishes, and taking care of Margie, who was small. Before sweeping I had to tuck up the mosquito nets that hung over the beds. These were large nets made of cheese cloth, which hung over each bed and fitted snuggly around the mattresses to keep out the mosquitoes. They were hung from the ceilings by a nail and strings and were let down over the beds about early nightfall. Many years later Mama still had those nets but had no more use for them. I took them and used them in a quilt that I still have today. The nets were very soft after many years of washing and were perfect in the middle of my quilt instead of the usual cotton batting.

That same summer I found Mama's old history book and read it from cover to cover. I remember doing my chores fast each morning just so I could read in the history book. It was all so fascinating to me. Mama came in from the field each day about eleven o'clock to cook dinner. I helped her with the cooking and then set the table.

All our clothes were washed by hand at every place we lived. This required a large cast iron pot in which to heat the water for washing and a big tub of warm water for rinsing. We used a bar of yellow laundry soap and a rub board to scrub them. This entire procedure took place outside near the pot over an open fire and as close to the water pump and clothesline as possible. White clothes sometimes required extra care, boiling in the pot with a tiny bit of lye. If the water was hard with chemicals of iron and magnesium, it meant that we used rainwater for washing the white clothes in order to keep them as white as possible. Chemicals in the water would turn them yellow. Some places we lived had soft water; others did not. We caught rainwater all those years at the Hatch place and used it for our white clothes. The clothes were rung out by hand after being rinsed then hung on the clothesline to dry. In the wintertime the clothes would freeze almost as fast as they were hung up. I still have the three-legged cast iron pot that Daddy bought in 1935 and used so many years in the country. It is in my backyard in Camden, Arkansas, where I use it for planting some of my flowers each year.

Washing dishes in that hard water meant we had very little suds. Each dish had to be rubbed with the soapy cloth and then rinsed. I remember washing dishes at school in my home economics class and telling Mama that it was a pleasure there because the water was soft and the suds made the chore easier.

In the fall of 1937, I started the fifth grade in the same school with Myrtis and a new student, Opal Plunkett. That year we studied American history, which I thoroughly enjoyed. It seems that each time we studied American history, we never had time to get to WWI and the politics of that era. Of course, Mama's history book, which I'd read previously, may have been written before WWI. That December of 1937 was the first time since I had been in school that we had not moved.

We were told that when we returned to school next semester, we would be using ink. I looked forward to that new experience. Times were still hard, so I did not expect much, if anything, for Christmas. Knowing by that age that there was no Santa Claus, I had requested to play Santa for my little sister Margie. I told my parents that I had learned in school that children in Holland received their gifts in their shoes, which they placed outside their bedroom doors. But I placed Margie's small gifts under the tree as usual, and after she opened them I went to my room to put on my shoes. There in one shoe was my fountain pen. The pen used ink from a bottle and was filled with a small lever on the side to suck up the ink into the rubber bladder from the bottle. I thought I was almost grown up! That spring in 1938 I passed to the sixth grade.

BROOMCORN

Mama saw an advertisement for broomcorn seed in a farm magazine that spring and sent for some. With the seed came instructions for making brooms. The seed looked like the birdseed we buy now for our songbirds. She planted it and it grew throughout the summer months until it was mature. She cut it to make a broom, which looked very much like the store-bought brooms and worked just as well. The songbird seed of today may be a byproduct of the factory-made brooms or vice versa.

That same spring we had an early Easter. Shortly afterward, my sister Margie got whooping cough. This was prior to the vaccine for whooping cough, and Margie became very ill. Mama had seen children with this disease before and knew it was serious. She had already lost two children and could not bare the thought of possibly losing another. I was only eleven years old at the time and do not remember if Margie saw a doctor, but she gradually overcame her illness.

Whooping cough was as common a disease in those days for small children as were measles and mumps. We were all so very glad when she recovered.

Mama had taken Margie the year before to the local schoolhouse where a parish health doctor came to give children's vaccinations. She had walked three miles, carrying Margie in her arms because she knew how important the immunization was. Margie got the two-in-one shot for diphtheria and typhoid, but it was not until some years later that the whooping cough vaccine was available.

Later that spring Mama and I chopped cotton together. She had hired a colored girl, Ginger, to watch Margie, who was only two years old. Ginger was about nine or ten years old at the time but was very dependable. She was the daughter of Tamar, a friend of Mama's from her early married life in the community. They were so glad to see each other after all those years. Mama paid Ginger with milk for babysitting Margie. It was a pleasant arrangement.

In the summertime the Methodist Church had a Bible School. The school teacher, Mrs. Mhoon Hatch, would come to pick us up for Bible school. This was a new experience for me, and I enjoyed it very much. In talking with some of the other children there, I met an older girl who attended school at Mangham. I told her that I had decided to not go to school anymore after the fifth grade because of several reasons. I felt I should stay out of school in the spring to chop cotton and then help pick it in the fall. I didn't want to get behind in school again because it was hard to catch up after missing. She encouraged me to stay in school and stated that the teachers would work with me in my studies and that I would like school. Mary LeSourd McIntosh was her name, and I later saw her in Columbia after I graduated from Mangham, while I was working at the courthouse. We were surprised to see each other there. I am certainly glad she had encouraged me to finish school.

It was that summer that Daddy and I both were ill with malaria at different times. Daddy was sick first and took quinine several weeks and recovered. Later I became ill and was taking quinine, but my fever became so high that I was incoherent. Mama was frightened by this and was very glad when I began to recover. Even though we slept under nets, the mosquitoes managed to bite us in the late afternoons near dark before we went to bed.

During the years at the Hatch place, we also raised goats. The cow pasture had lots of briars, as well as small haw trees that were preventing growth of grass for the cows to graze. The goats loved the briars and soon had them under control. We would chop down the haw trees and leave them hanging onto the stump. They continued to sprout out leaves for quite a while. The goats climbed over the hanging trees and nibbled them off. Thus the goats had food and made a better pasture for the cows. The goats hung around under a big oak tree in the pasture near our house. The little kids scampered and climbed over blocks of wood that had been left under the tree. It was so much fun to watch their antics. These were brush goats, which were not for milking. Daddy did kill some of the young goats; he dressed them and sold them to the neighbors. We sometimes kept a little for our own use. Mama baked a hind quarter and made some dressing. All of us except Daddy enjoyed this different meat.

That fall of 1938 I entered Mangham School in the sixth grade. I rode the school bus about twenty miles to school each way. My teacher there was Mrs. Elsie Bell Terral. Mr. Mike Bell, her father, was a well known plantation owner. Mrs. Terral was married to a doctor, Forrest Terral, who later had a practice in Lake Providence. Mrs. Terral was a very good teacher, who treated the sixth graders as young adults and taught us responsibility. Mangham School was a big school and had two sixth grade classrooms. Each classroom had thirty-eight to forty students.

There was a school cafeteria, but I could not afford the lunches, so I took my own. During nice weather students who took their lunches were allowed to eat outside under the pecan trees; but during cold or rainy weather, we ate indoors. I did well in school that year and enjoyed what I learned. We had our regular readers, as well as some books with short stories and comprehension questions to answer afterward. This enabled me to improve my reading skills so much that I was reading on a tenth grade level before school was out that year.

My favorite subject that year was geography, and

I especially enjoyed learning the countries of Europe and their capitals. Naturally the countries of Europe, as well as countries in other continents, have changed many times since. It was during the fall of the sixth grade that we studied the news about Nazi Germany's aggression toward Austria and Czechoslovakia. We knew that was an important event—and tragic—but we did not realize how this would later impact the entire world.

On December 18, 1938, my little sister Sarah Suzanne was born. Now Mama had two little children at home, and I was a big help to her. Being ten years older than Margie and twelve years older than Sue (as we often called Suzanne), I was more of a mother figure to them than a sister. After I married, my first daughter, Linda, got my sisters' names mixed up. She always heard our mama call them on a number of occasions, "Margie, Sue, come here." It was after Linda began to talk that she called each of them "Marre-Sue" for a while.

It was about February 1939 when I became ill with measles. I was twelve years old at the time and became sick enough that I missed quite a few days of school. The day I was able to go back to school happened to be picture day. Needless to say my pictures did not look very good, because I did not yet feel good. I went home that day and began to get sick again. This time I showed signs of chicken pox and was out of school for at least a week or more. I did not see the doctor for either of these illnesses, but having them so close together was

difficult. I was unable to do my schoolwork while I had
measles but returned to school as soon as I recovered.

A Community Tragedy

In the spring of 1939, the Arice Golden family came to have Easter dinner with our family. It was a very warm April, and the spring grass had come out. That afternoon we had a warm, hard rain, which left many puddles of clear water over the grass. We children were allowed to take off our shoes to wade barefoot in the puddles. The Goldens had come to our house by a shortcut through the fields on the turn-rows. They knew that going home would be muddy, so they spent the night. It must have rained a lot more during the night because the river was very high the next day.

As was told to us later, about the time the Golden family reached the Hatch Bridge, they saw the Plunket children and two other neighbors on the bridge looking at the fast-rolling river. Opal, being the oldest of those children, had her little brother Aaron in her arms with three little sisters following close behind. At that point they heard a car coming, and the children were told to move to the rail of the bridge. This bridge was made of heavy one foot wooden planks that crossed metal rails, with two metal runways on top of the planks for car tires. Unfortunately, it was an old bridge and was decaying and had some holes. Billie Jean, the smallest little girl, stepped backward and fell through one of those holes.

Despite all efforts to save her, she was immediately swept away and disappeared from the sight of those on the bridge. It was several days before her body was recovered. This was another sad time for our family. We had crossed that bridge many times, and I had crossed it some on horseback. Everyone was very careful after that time to watch for the holes. It was many years later that the old bridge was replaced.

That same spring was the only time I chopped cotton alone. Daddy was busy plowing, and Mama was nursing a small baby and also had a two-year-old in the house. She had to milk the cows twice daily and do the housework, pump the water, do all the cooking, and care for the garden. Daddy did the fieldwork of plowing and planting, so I chopped cotton that spring when I was not at school. I completed the task on June 22, my thirteenth birthday. Despite missing a lot of school that spring while sick with the measles, I was able to pass to the seventh grade.

Margie, & Sue, 1939 at the Hatch place

Daddy learned in 1939 that one of our neighbors, Mr. Will Froust, had a syrup mill. We wanted to plant sugarcane that year, but we did not have the seed cane because it had to be bought the year before and bedded down over the winter. That was the year Daddy planted sorghum and we made sorghum syrup; however, we decided we did not like the syrup from sorghum, so he planted sugarcane from then on. Daddy bought some sugarcane stalks and bedded them down in the fall as seed, dug them up in the spring, and planted them in rows. The cane stalks had eyes at each joint, which grew into a new stalk the next year. The next fall we had sugarcane to take to the syrup mill. We did this about three years, and then Mr. Froust moved.

Lillian, age 13, stripping sorghum for the mill

I entered the seventh grade at Mangham in the fall, and my teacher was Miss Bessie Noble. That year we began to study current events, so I was introduced to Weekly Readers. We learned about the British king's abdication of the throne when he married a commoner. On a more serious note, Poland was invaded by Nazi Germany, and WWII began in Europe. We did not have a radio at home or get a newspaper, so the only news we had of the war in Europe was by word of mouth from neighbors or what I learned at school. Everything we heard about the Nazis was bad, but it was only after the Allied invasion that we learned the horrific facts.

It was about this time that *Gone with the Wind* was released. I did not get to see the movie until many years later—after I was married and a mother. I do remember seeing in the Sears, Roebuck catalog a picture of a dress made from a material advertised as similar to a dress worn by Vivian Leigh in that movie. It was a green, leafy print that was pretty but too expensive for us to purchase.

During the summer of 1940, when I was fourteen years old, my sister Suzanne, who was only eighteen months old, became ill. She had a high fever and diarrhea and was very listless. When she was taken to the pediatrician in Monroe, he said she had dysentery. He prescribed medicine and a special diet. Mama was relieved when Suzanne began to improve, as she was most concerned having already lost one baby to dysentery. It was especially hard for children living in the country to get medical attention if their parents did not have a car or truck. Few, if any, of the sharecroppers had their own vehicles. We were very grateful to our neighbors who shared their transportation with us.

It was that fall when I was first included in the syrup making. I was privileged to have the job of feeding the stalks of sugarcane into the crusher at the mill. A mule furnished the power as it walked around in a circle, pulling the arm that turned the cylinders that squeezed the juice from the cane. It was poured into a long copper pan called an evaporator that sat over a fire where the syrup was cooked. Daddy was the one who skimmed the syrup and also kept the fire regulated. Mr. Froust watched the process carefully and decided when the syrup was just right to be drawn off. Daddy sure did enjoy the syrup, as did we all. It was fortunate that we were able to raise the cane and have syrup made because we could not have afforded to purchase it.

Lillian's oil painting of syrup mill. She is the one feeding the cane into the press.

Times had been very hard for most country people and farmers during the Depression years. It had been hard for poor people who lived in the towns and cities as well, but I did not know of that life. I imagine many town people were out of work and had a very hard time feeding their families. At least we farm families were able to raise a lot of our food. Keeping the food fresh was another problem. We did not have a refrigerator, not only because we did not have electricity, but we could not have afforded one. An ice box did not require electricity, but we did not live near a highway with ice delivery. People who lived in the country on the roads that had ice delivery had ice boxes and received blocks of ice several times a week as needed and as they could afford. We were not so fortunate.

Also at that time, the catalogs began to show the electric appliances that were becoming available during the rural electrification of the country. However, it had not reached our area. The landlords did not wire tenants' houses for electricity even if it was available. One of the things I remember about the catalog was seeing many electrical appliances that would do so many of the things we had to do by hand. What a dream come true I thought it would be if I ever had some of those appliances.

It was many years later that my parents had electricity in their home; my husband wired the house for light bulbs in each room in 1946. The first electric appliance Mama got was a refrigerator. It was so nice for her to have a cold place to keep her milk and butter.

Daddy soon bought a small radio and an electric iron. Before that we had no way of hearing news except through school or neighbors who told us. Mama had always ironed with a heavy flatiron that she heated on the wood stove. That was how I had ironed my school clothes all through the years I was home.

Many of our everyday chores were not easy by any means; but we had a good family life and knew hard work was the only way to get things done. Mama often sang as she worked because she must have felt that made the work easier and more pleasant. I remember many times hearing Mama as she worked in the house singing, "Let others see Jesus in you. Let others see Jesus in you. Keep telling the story, be faithful and true. Let others see Jesus in you." Sometimes she sang "Jesus, Jesus, how I trust him! How I've proved him o'er and o'er. Jesus, Jesus, precious Jesus, O for grace to trust him more." These were two of her favorite choruses from hymns.

HIGH SCHOOL

High school for us in those days started in eighth grade because we had only eleven grades total for completion and graduation. I missed the first six weeks of high school in 1940 because I helped the family pick cotton. The teachers understood the situation, as I probably was not the only student needed at home during cotton-picking time. I studied hard the next grading period and soon caught up with the class. I don't remember how much school I missed in those years due to helping on the farm, but I do know I continued to help after school each day, on weekends as much as possible, and each summer. My parents encouraged me to stay in school because they knew the importance of education since they had not been able to finish high school.

We were required to take three years of math, four years of English, two years of history and two years of science to graduate. Every girl was also required to take home economics. Our principal insisted all girls learn those skills whether they lived on a farm or in town. Each boy was required to take agricultural courses. Each student was also required to have physical education. Besides those required subjects, I also took typing and shorthand. Other electives included bookkeeping, music, physics, and Latin; but I did not take any of those courses.

One Monday morning in December 1941, on the way to school on the bus, everyone was talking about our country being at war. The Japanese had bombed Pearl Harbor the day before. Most of us did not know where Pearl Harbor was. I knew that Europe was involved in a war and knew that the United States was an ally of the British, but I had not thought that our country might actually become a part of the war. We did not have a radio at home and had not been able to keep up with world affairs. The Depression years had just begun to take a turn for better times when here came the beginning of four more very hard years.

It was not too long before many items were rationed. These included tires, gasoline, shoes, and a number of food items, such as sugar, coffee, butter, and shortening. Rationing of tires and gasoline did not affect us as much as families with cars, nor did rationing of butter and shortening, because we had our own on the farm. Rationing of coffee did not affect us much because we did not drink much coffee—only for breakfast. Even though shoes were rationed, we were accustomed to purchasing only what we needed. The sugar ration was sufficient for our needs. The ration books were issued to each member of the family with stamps inside for various items. Our family often had stamps left over in our ration books.

I still have one of my ration books that survived all these years through many moves. This book was one I had taken with me when I left home because I had been told restaurants would ask me for some of my stamps. I was never asked for my stamps, so they have survived. Perhaps that was because I did not eat many of the rationed items, such as coffee or sweets. Some of them were used when my landlady offered to help me make divinity candy. I purchased sugar a number of times for this purpose. I also made a fruitcake for Christmas in that way.

Ration Book

Ration Book

Making do with what we had was not a new idea to our family. During the war years we often heard and saw a popular slogan: use it up, wear it out, make it do, or do without. Mama had believed strongly in this philosophy before the slogan became well publicized. She had taught us girls to be frugal in this way in our daily lives. We used feed sacks to make some of the items we needed, such as sheets and hand towels. The material was coarsely woven white cotton with some printing. We washed and bleached them, and after several washings they became softer.

Another example of Mama's ingenuity was to use leftover shingles to build chicken coops on an a-frame design for her brooder hens. These were shingles Daddy had made to roof a pole barn he had also made. The shingles were made from short lengths of cypress logs by riving with a froe. A froe is a tool about twelve or fourteen inches long with a handle attached at a right angle. The blade is wedge-shaped, thick on the top edge with a dull bevel on the splitting edge. It is used to cleave (or rive) various types of wood. A wooden mallet was used to pound the blade of the froe to split the wood. Mama often used nails that she had saved from tearing down old structures. We always saved the nails and straightened them out for use again even before the nail shortage during the war.

As soon as all the chicks were hatched, we would put them with their mother in the coop. The coop was always placed on a well-drained spot in the backyard. Each coop had a sliding door made with a shingle, and Mama would leave a small place for the chicks to come out into the sun early in the morning. In this way the chicks stayed close to the coop and did not wander off into the wet grass, which was not good for them. After the dew dried on the grass, the mama hen was released to take her brood around the yard to scratch and feed them. Even though we had fed the chicks and hen when they were released, they enjoyed gathering their own bugs and insects. The chicks followed mama hen and stayed together and answered her call. When evening came she returned to her coop with her brood and went inside for the night, and we shut the door. At various times we had three or four broods of chicks at different ages. Each hen knew her coop, and each chick knew its mama. They were so cute, and we always enjoyed the families of little chicks.

It was at some point in my high school years, after our country was at war, that my sister Margie became ill again. She was about five years old, and Mama was very concerned. Someone in the community took her and my parents to the doctor nearest, who was in Alto. He said she had pneumonia and gave her some medicine. When they returned home, Mama was crying because she was fearful Margie would die from pneumonia, as children often did in those days. I reassured Mama that pneumonia was not as dangerous as it once was because of the new sulfa drugs that had come into use. We had heard about these new *wonder drugs* when reading at school about war injuries. Mama was very relieved to hear this, and Margie quickly recovered. So even though there were many inconveniences to Americans during the war, there were some good things discovered during those years.

One summer in my early high school years, a man selling two wild horses from the open western plains came by our farm. Daddy wanted both horses and traded yearlings for them. We named the white female Dolly and the red male Dan. Dan was too small for us to ride, but Dolly was large, and I wanted to gentle her to ride like Black Beauty, our present saddle horse. One day when Daddy was not home, I decided to begin her training. I went into the barn lot and managed to get a rope over her head, but unfortunately it settled down close to her shoulders, which made it impossible for me to restrain her.

Over the fence she went, rope and all, with me

pulling as hard as I could. To my horror there she was in open pasture dragging the rope, and I had no way to catch her. Also to my horror, I had extremely bad rope burns on both hands. Mama did what she could to take care of my injury, but the worst part was telling Daddy when he got home that Dolly was loose in the pasture and dragging a rope. He did not scold me too much because he saw that I was suffering with burned hands. He managed to catch her, and she gradually gentled down.

A few years later when Dolly had a young colt that was nursing, there was a child in the community who was very sick with whooping cough. Someone had told the child's parents that mare's milk was very good for whooping cough. They came to our farm because they knew we had a mare with a foal. Mama was very willing in any way she could to help this sick child. Someone held Dolly with her foal nearby while Mama milked her. It was only a small amount, but they said it helped a lot, and the child recovered. Many years later I found out that homogenized milk would soothe an irritated throat. Later I read somewhere that mare's milk is homogenized!

In 1943 we went back to visit Grandpa Judy where he was living in a tent on Mr. Bill Ray's place. He had made the tent himself and added a stick-and-dirt chimney. Grandpa was very independent and seemed quite content. He was seventy-nine by that time and no longer farming. He was having some health problems, so we invited him to come live with us, which he did.

Sometime soon afterward he and Daddy built a boat out of cypress lumber. Grandpa had the knowledge, and Daddy did the work. It was about three feet wide and sixteen feet long. It had a seat back and front and one across the middle. The bottom boards fit tightly, and when it was put into the water it did not leak. We lived about one-half mile from the Boeuf River at that time, so it was left tied to a tree near the bank. Daddy used it to cross the river to visit neighbors for a while, but it was soon stolen. I remember watching them make the boat one summer, but soon it was time to return to school.

Mangham High was a large school serving Richland Parish but not the only high school. Rayville High was larger. Both schools had football teams and were arch rivals. The Mangham Dragons and Rayville Hornets played each other in football and basketball. Our classrooms contained thirty-eight to forty students each. After the United States entered the war in December 1941, our classes were somewhat smaller, as many of the boys joined the different branches of the service and some students left school for other reasons. Our freshman class had close to eighty students that fall, but by May of 1944, we had only forty graduates. Of those, at least three-fourths were girls. An acquaintance of mine was married to a serviceman, but she stayed in school and graduated. We focused on our classes, not talking much about the war, and keeping our minds on our studies in order to finish school.

Mr. T.A. Judd was our principal at Mangham.

He taught algebra and geometry and took care of administrative duties. My favorite subject, home economics, was taught by Mrs. Adam Childress. This included both sewing and cooking. Miss Virgie Evans was my teacher for general science and chemistry. My English and literature teacher for three years was Mrs. Christine McConnell. Miss Ola Cooper taught history and biology. Mr. Rushing taught general math. Mrs. McElwain was the business teacher who taught me typing, but when she left Mrs. Thelmaline Jones became the business teacher and taught me shorthand.

My junior year our classmates sponsored the junior/senior banquet, and in turn our senior class was honored with a banquet. There were no dances or proms as they are known today. During the war years all resources were prioritized for the war effort. Our school was unable to have a class annual during those years due to the diversion of paper to the war effort. Naturally there was a shortage of gasoline and tires, as well as many foods. These shortages curtailed many normal school activities during this time until the war was over.

My grades were good enough for me to be inducted into the Mu Sigma Honor Society. There was no banquet for the honor society that year, but we were each given a pin. In my senior year our class took a trip to the national park in Vicksburg, Mississippi. School buses were not allowed to be used for this extracurricular activity, so we obtained and paid for a cattle truck to take us to the park, which was close enough for a day trip. We took our own lunch. We had a nice tour of the grounds and buildings and learned about the battle of Vicksburg during the War between the States.

My only other extracurricular activity was the senior play. There were no tryouts for the play, but Mrs. Christine McConnell, one of the senior sponsors, chose the players. She selected me for one of the lead characters, Mrs. Updyke, a snooty matron. I don't remember the name of the play nor much about it. I do know that Mrs. McConnell felt that those people chosen for the play could do a good job while maintaining their grades. She also had to consider how those chosen would get to play practice in the evenings. Stanley Douciere lived at the far end of the bus route and had access to a car, so he picked up three other students, including me, for play practice.

The play was a success and I enjoyed it, but I did not pursue acting afterward. Many years later when asked what she remembered about my high school years, my sister Margie made the remark that she wondered how I knew how to portray a *snooty* person in the senior play. Margie had just been eight years old at the time of the play, so she must have been impressed by my performance. My younger sister Sue remembers riding home from the play on the school bus. The school buses ran their regular rural routes so families could attend the senior play, which was an important event. The funds raised from ticket sales for the play were used by the senior class to purchase and erect a rather large monument on the school grounds. This monument honored all our young men who had gone off to serve in the military.

Up until graduation I had not given any thought to what I might do after high school because my primary goal for those years had been just to graduate. I heard some other young people on the bus on the way home talking about their future plan to get into Western Union Training School in Springfield, Missouri. Right away I knew that opportunity was just what I needed and wanted. It seemed to me that it was my only chance to make a place for myself in the future.

PROSPECT OF A NEW LIFE

Some of our classmates went on to college. I did not have the opportunity to attend college but was fortunate enough to hear about the school in Missouri for Western Union telegraph operators. Four of us from the 1944 graduating class of Mangham High went to Springfield to begin our studies at the Western Union school. Sarah Margaret Joyner, Shirley McIntyre, Elvy Roberts, and I all took the test for entrance there in Monroe, Louisiana. Once we passed the test we were given passes for travel on the train from Monroe to Springfield.

Upon our arrival at school, we were reimbursed for our meals while traveling and our first night's stay in a hotel. New students were then placed in rooming houses. When I had left home, Grandpa Judy gave me his pocket watch so that I might always be on time. I appreciated the gift very much and had that watch for many years. He also advised me to make sure that I was not to room on the second floor because he had heard recently of a fire in a building where people on the upper floors had died because they could not get out.

Sarah Margaret and I roomed together in a private home near a teacher's college. We could not help but notice the young male military personnel who attended that college. These cadets were quite a sight while marching and drilling in their uniforms. We usually ate breakfast at the College Inn, a small diner across from the college. We used the city bus to get to classes each day and ate our lunch at the nearby YWCA.

During the Western Union training classes, we had to learn a new keyboard system unlike the typewriters we were used to, more like computer keyboards today. Telegrams were sent in all capital letters, and we could not see what we were typing. The words printed out on strips of gummed tape, which came from a machine across the room. We learned how to take those strips of tape with the messages and feed them neatly through a tube where they were moistened. Then we pasted the messages carefully to a telegram sheet.

There were many other things to learn about typing and gumming messages in the proper priority; learning the various signals from bells that were rung on the machine and making sure top priority government messages received immediate attention. Many of the routine messages were to and from various businesses closely connected with the war effort. These included railroads, chemical companies, lumber companies, and others. When a government message was coming in, bells would ring, signaling different priorities. If five bells rang, the operator had to immediately stop what she was doing and accept that message and make sure it was delivered. One example would be the death notification of a serviceman.

There was a lot to learn in those eight weeks, and we stayed very busy each school day. We attended classes Monday through Friday but had our evenings and weekends free. Sarah Margaret and I attended church every Sunday at a large Baptist church downtown. I always sent my church bulletin to Mama with a short letter each week to let her know I was attending church. Mailing a letter took three cents. Coincidentally, years later Sarah Margaret lived in Bastrop with her husband during the time my husband and I lived there. They attended Van Avenue Baptist Church where we also attended, and our children went to school together. It was Sarah Margaret Lambert who led my older daughter, Linda, to a saving knowledge of Christ while she attended Sunbeams in the Lambert home.

Each of us received sixteen dollars weekly during the school, out of which came our room rent, our meals, and bus fare. The rooms cost us about two dollars and fifty cents weekly per person. Meals were chosen carefully, but we could eat for about twenty-five cents at breakfast and thirty-five or forty cents at lunch. Evening meals were at various places and a little more expensive. We often ate sandwiches at a drugstore and sometimes purchased sandwich food to make our own in the basement-kitchen of the rooming house.

On Saturday nights we often went to a movie,

which cost only twenty-five cents. Some of the ladies in our rooming house who were students at the college had a car. I can remember going with them to the city park on several occasions. Sometimes we dated some of the cadets from the college. They were all very polite and well-behaved.

That experience during my training for Western Union was a very pleasant one, and the opportunity was extremely fortunate for me. Upon completion of the course, we were given a certificate and reported back to Monroe at the Western Union office. At that time we were assigned to our first offices, and I went to Minden, Louisiana, near Shreveport. I took the bus to Minden.

My office manager there, Mary Frances Pirtle, found me a room nearby. This first job increased my pay about two dollars per week and lasted about nine months. When Miss Pirtle left the office, my new manager was Mr. W.W. Haggarty. Many years later while living in Bastrop, my older daughter worked at the local welfare office with Mary Frances Pirtle, and my younger daughter attended school with her nephew.

During my last few years at home as I had attended the Pentecostal church, I realized that I was not saved. That was, to me, a very disturbing condition. I knew God's commandments and tried to keep them. I knew the golden rule and tried to live by it. But I knew I was not strong enough in my own strength. I did not know what to do; however, I did not ask anyone, not even

Mama. I just pushed it to the back of my mind and tried not to dwell on it too much.

When I moved to Minden, the problem was solved. I began attending First Baptist Church and Sunday school. There my Sunday school teacher explained to me that if I believed in Jesus, that he was God's son, that he was the Christ, the Savior, and that he died on the cross for my sins, and if I repented of my sins and desired to follow Christ the rest of my life, I would be saved that instant!

I was so overjoyed that I wept uncontrollably. To think of all those years I had worried, and rightly so! If I had only known how simple it was to have eternal security! Now I knew I would be in heaven someday instead of that terrible place called hell. At that point I could not speak through my tears of joy, but when my dear teacher asked me if I did believe in Jesus Christ and wanted to follow him, I nodded my head. I rejoiced and joined the church that very day and was baptized the next Sunday night. My baptism was to show my obedience to Christ and to represent my rebirth in him.

I have learned through my entire life, and am still learning, how Jesus helps me cope with life's ups and downs, gladness and sorrows, illnesses and health. I also know that this life is only temporary, and the life afterward is eternal happiness with my Savior. Of course, I have not lived a perfect life, as no one can, but I know my sins are covered by Christ's shed blood. I have felt close to him and tried my best to live for him ever since that day I accepted him. I feel that he has watched over me and my family and given us many blessings through the years.

Lillian, Spring 1945 in Minden

NEW BEGINNINGS

I was in Minden for almost a year and was then transferred to Bastrop in May of 1945 to attend managerial school. It was a four-week course taught by Mrs. Tommy Thompkins in the Western Union office. During that time I stayed at the McBride Boardinghouse on Washington Street with another Western Union employee. We had breakfast and lunch there family style. The school was several blocks away, but we were dismissed long enough to go back to the boardinghouse for lunch. For the evening meal we usually ate a light meal in a local diner or restaurant. That training allowed us to manage a small office when we left. My roommate went to Boxite, Arkansas, and I went to Pocahontas, Arkansas, where I managed a small office for a month. From there I relieved an operator for vacation in Blytheville, Arkansas. Then I did the same thing in Jonesboro, Arkansas.

In August of 1945, I was transferred to a large Western Union office in Alexandria, Louisiana, for only two weeks to relieve an operator for vacation. It was between these assignments that I took my own vacation. I took a bus from Jonesboro to Shreveport, Louisiana, where I had made prior arrangements to visit a friend who was stationed at the Barksdale Base in Bossier City. Hal Parker was his name, and he was from Boston, Massachusetts. I had met him when I was working in Minden. He had invited me at that time to an open house on the base where he worked. I had enjoyed my previous visit to the base where I had tried out the military page-printer, their form of telegraph communication. I thought it would be nice to visit him again.

I was met by Hal at the bus station, and he took me to the guest house on base where he had arranged for me to stay two nights. He had some time off and showed me around the base. We went swimming one day at the base pool. One morning we ate breakfast at the chow hall. Hal was a parachute instructor, so he showed me how his trainees jumped off a tall tower in their training by actually making a jump himself. When he was preparing to jump, he checked every buckle and strap several times. He told me that no matter how many times a jumper checked his gear, he always wanted to check it one more time.

Hal took me to the bus station for my trip home for a visit. A neighbor brought Daddy to the Monroe bus station to meet me. I had a nice visit at home with my family before my new assignment in Alexandria, Louisiana. There I stayed in a rooming house, which meant I had to eat all my meals out. It was there that I gained experience on the money order desk. One day in August of 1945, I was at the front counter when I looked up and realized the entire area between me and the front door was absolutely packed with customers.

As it turned out, the pandemonium was due to the fact that an atom bomb had been dropped on Japan. We could barely take the customers' money fast enough to get all their telegrams accepted. Our office manager called every available person to the counter to handle the rush. Most customers were soldiers sending messages to their families back home. The only telegram that stands out in my memory was one from an elderly man who appeared to have been weeping who had a message for the president.

I had been instructed to always clear any telegram for the president through my supervisor. The supervisor read the telegram, which stated that the man was sorry that the bomb had not been dropped sooner so that it might have prevented the loss of his son's life. I was told that there was nothing wrong with the telegram and to send it. The wide street in front of the Western Union office was jammed the rest of the day with traffic and pedestrians weaving their way across. I can't remember how long the bedlam lasted, but I knew at the time that this dramatic event was a turning point in history.

A Better Life

A few days after that momentous event, I was transferred to Columbia, Louisiana, which was only a short distance from where my parents lived. They had moved from the Hatch place to Mrs. Mabel Pritchard's farm. Daddy was still sharecropping. Columbia is a small town in Caldwell Parish, about twenty-eight miles south of Monroe.

This assignment was different in that the Western Union desk was in a drugstore and did not have a trained employee handling the telegrams until I got there. As untrained operators, the druggists were having much difficulty and had requested a trained employee. Shortly afterward I terminated my employment with Western Union and agreed to work for the drugstore manager as a clerk for him, as well as handle the Western Union desk. It was for about the same pay but allowed me to stay in Columbia closer to my family, and I didn't have to move all the time.

One day while eating breakfast at the counter in

a small café on the courthouse square, I overheard a young man talking about hard times and attending law school. He was sitting just two stools down from me. I heard him say his name was John McKeithen, and I recognized the family name. All families had been affected in one way or another during the Depression, and the war had prevented many young men from following their original plans for their lives. I do know for a fact that young John J. McKeithen finished law school, and that he became Governor of Louisiana in 1964. He was from Grayson, just south of Columbia, and had a brother who was a doctor in Columbia. I would also meet that brother later in my life.

It was there while I was working in Columbia that I met a young cocky sailor requesting an extension on his leave from the navy. I explained to him that he would not receive the extension without a good reason, but he insisted that I send his telegram. Naturally his request was denied.

E.B. Duff, Jr., 20 years old in the Solomon Islands, 1943

When I got to my room that evening, I saw that handsome sailor again while he visited with several young ladies in the backyard at the rooming house. I did not go outside but wrote a letter to my mother that night stating that "I have met my man."

I didn't see that sailor for a while, but in January of 1946 there he was back at my desk. He was in civilian clothes, and I almost didn't recognize him. He did not have a telegram that time but wanted to chat with me. He didn't ask me out that day, but pretty soon we were keeping company almost every evening. He took me to movies sometimes, but a lot of our time together was spent driving in his dad's car then parking so we could talk and get to know each other.

E.B. & Lillian, Jan. 1946 in Columbia, Louisiana on the Ouachita River

In February after we had dated awhile, E.B. began his studies at school in New Orleans at Soulé Business College. He was attending there on the GI Bill as many other veterans were doing. About that time a friend and I made a visit to see my family where they where sharecropping on the Duchesne (pronounced Du'chan) place in Richland Parish. As it turned out, this was the last place they lived as sharecroppers. My friend Rose O'leta Watts took several pictures of me and my family that day. It was also about this time that I accepted a job as secretary in the Agricultural Extension Office at the Caldwell Parish Courthouse.

Lillian, Spring 1946

Clarence, Eliza, Lillian, Margie, and Sue

It was the fifth of May that same year that E.B. Duff Jr. and I were married in Columbia by Dr. Guy Winstead at the First Baptist Church. Many years later after we had been married about thirty years, I overheard E.B. tell someone that after he had met me only once, he went back to his navy assignment telling his buddies that he had been all around the world, but while on leave in his hometown he had met the girl he would marry.

It was in June that I joined him in New Orleans and returned to work with Western Union. Due to cutbacks in Western Union offices, I was let go and then worked for a short time in the Tulane shirt factory.

We lived a very frugal life there during our first few months of marriage. It was there that our first child was conceived. For a while we lived in a rooming house but soon rented a small apartment on Canal Street. We took the trolley cars to work and school each day. This was my first opportunity to use my cooking skills on my husband. E.B. must have been pleased because his weight jumped from 130 pounds to 160 pounds that first month.

Back on Boeuf River in North Louisiana, my family had a surprise visitor. It was my Grandpa Judy's niece Anna Edgemon from South Carolina. I was unable to meet her, but her visit was special to my family because they were not often able to be with relatives. I am so glad that we have a picture to record that special occasion.

Grandpa Asbury J. Judy, 1946, with niece Anna Edgemon; Margie, age 12, Sue, age 10

We returned to Columbia in November 1946 because my father-in-law had a heart attack and needed E.B. to help in the family business. We lived with his parents, Bowden and Lucille, in their home on Lakeside Street at the foot of the Columbia hill. He was parts manager at James and Duff Motor Company.

Linda Louise was born in June the next year. In fact she was born on the twenty-eighth, my father's birthday, and Dr. McKeithen delivered her. We had been living with E.B.'s parents while E.B. helped his daddy in the business. My sister-in-law, Eva, had married Herbert Haddox, a cousin to my fourth grade school teacher. Eva and Herbert were living in Ward 5 on his daddy's farm in the community where I had lived as a child. After a short while we rented a duplex on Pearl Street at the foot of the levee of Ouachita River. When Linda was only ten months old, Bowden had another heart attack while driving his car. That accident took his life.

After his dad's death, the business was dissolved, and he worked for a while with a construction company digging out Bayou Lafouche. Then he took a job in Pennsylvania working as a millwright, building a generator for Westinghouse. He later worked in Natchez, Mississippi, as an auto mechanic. He also worked in Shreveport in the construction of the airport. From there he went to Lake Charles and again worked in construction, this time building a runway for an airport to be called Chenault Field. Heavy rains covered the area with fifteen feet of water, so the project was abandoned.

Linda, age 3, with Grandma Eliza in 1950

We returned to Columbia in 1950 and lived again on Pearl Street, this time in a house we purchased. Shortly afterward, E.B.'s brother, Robert, was in a fatal automobile accident. E.B. assumed his brother's debt, which added to our financial strain.

It was in April of 1953 that our second daughter, Judy Katherine, was born, again while we were in Columbia. Dr. Carroll delivered Judy on Easter Sunday, the fifth of April. My regular doctor was Dr. Wren Causey, but he had gone to his home in Bewelcome, Mississippi, for Easter. When he returned he came to our hospital room and gave Judy a small brown New Testament inscribed to her from him. Judy told me years later that all three of her girls used that little testament as their first Bible.

Those first years of our life together were happy but somewhat difficult. In fact, a lot of our life together was filled with challenges and hard times as with most marriages. During those hard times I was able to use the skills I had learned on the farm. I gardened, I canned, and I sewed and took care of the home and children as we moved around. We had moved several times before 1953, and E.B. worked at many different jobs.

It was in the summer of that year that my husband accepted employment in Bastrop with International Paper Company. E.B. said it was time we settled down with a stable job so our children could feel secure and attend school without having to move so much. I agreed. Steady employment did not exactly put us on easy street because we had debts we were trying to pay off. One of the things I regret during that time is that we could not afford more pictures of Judy when she was little.

Judy, 6 months old in 1953

Our first small home was a rented house on Crossett Road without heat or indoor plumbing. We did have running cold water at the kitchen sink, but I had to heat all the water for washing and bathing on the electric stove. We used portable kerosene heaters in the daytime but not while we were sleeping. We did not have money for recreation, but E.B. enjoyed his hobby of raising bantam chickens. This gave us much pleasure, as well as eggs to eat. To supplement our income, E.B. took a job repairing television sets. He purchased his first black and white TV in 1953, as he very much enjoyed electronics. It was during this time that my parents had to leave farm life and move near us in Bastrop because of my father's stroke.

After two years of renting that house on the Crossett Road, E.B. was able to purchase two acres with a modest home just outside the city limits on

Bayou Bartholomew. Even though this house was very small and basic, we had indoor plumbing and good heating from gas heat. We cleared those two acres of cotton stalks and began planting grass. Later I was able to have a garden and plenty of flowerbeds. We planted pecan trees that later bore pecans for many years.

E.B.'s new hobby became astronomy, and he built several telescopes, grinding his own mirrors. The company that silvered those telescope mirrors told him that those were the most accurate homemade mirrors they had ever silvered. The twelve-inch telescope was the largest in the state at the time except one at LSU in Baton Rouge. The science teachers from the Bastrop schools often brought their students out on Friday nights for star-gazing parties. We had the perfect setting away from the lights of town. This was a happy time.

Eight years later E.B. purchased a much nicer home for us near the country club area of Bastrop. We moved on November 22, 1963, a sad day in American history. Our living conditions had certainly improved by this time. It was while we had lived on the Bayou that my father passed away, and now my mother came to live with us for a while. Both girls completed school while living here on Oakdale Street. Linda married, and her son was born while we lived there. She lived with us a short time before she took the baby and went to join her military husband in Germany in 1967.

We lived in Bastrop for eighteen years total before our move with IP to the mill at Springhill, Louisiana.

Judy was still at home with us a short time in Springhill but soon married and moved to Texas with her military husband. About that time Mama came to live with us again, this time because I had a heart attack. She was very helpful, and I soon recovered. Her extended stay allowed my husband to see Mama's real character of being very kind and mild-mannered, so he asked her to stay and make her home with us permanently. Mama and I gardened and quilted together. We lived in Springhill eight years before that paper mill closed and E.B. was transferred to Camden, Arkansas.

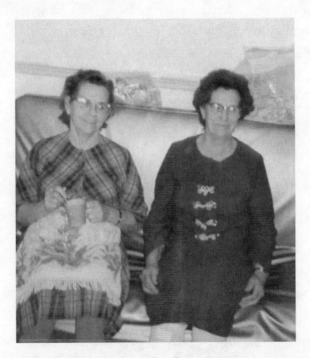

Eliza Laird & Iva Patrick, 1972

It was on Upper White Oak Lake near Chidester, outside Camden, that we purchased a house and lived for twenty-two years. Even though E.B. spent a lot of time in the paper mill before retirement, his spare time was now spent fishing and hunting. Mama had moved with us, so she and I had a large garden each summer and made many quilts during the winter months. What wonderful years we had together! We attended Chidester Baptist Church together, and she made many good friends there. It became necessary for her to enter a nursing home in 1987. She passed away in January 1992 at the age of eighty-nine. Even today, after sixteen years, I find myself wanting to tell her or share with her something that I have done the way she taught me.

Eliza Laird in 1990

Lillian, June 1995

E.B. had started with International Paper Company as a clerk-typist but moved up in the company to instrument foreman before his retirement. It turned out that E.B.'s employment with IP had been the real beginning of a better life for us and our children. There were a few rough years in Bastrop, but life improved through his promotions at the paper mills before he retired in 1985.

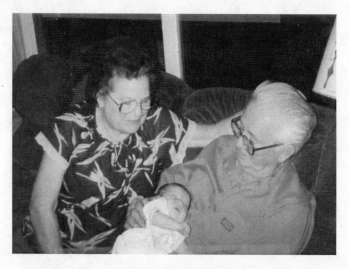

Lillian, E.B., with Great-granddaughter Suzanne Eliza
Kitchens, October, 1997

Our hard work and frugality allowed us to have a
lifestyle that was so much better than my years on the
farm as a sharecropper's daughter. We celebrated our
fiftieth anniversary in 1996, but four years later E.B.
was diagnosed with Alzheimer's. We found it necessary
to move into Camden, next door to Linda. He passed
away in November 2004. Again it was my faith that
helped me cope with those years during his illness. It
was a couple of years after E.B.'s death that I realized
as I walked through my modest but comfortable home
in Camden that my dream had long ago come true.

My dream as a teenager on the farm had been that I
might live in a house someday that did not have cracks
in the floor or walls, did not have a leaky roof or flies
and mosquitoes in and out the doors. My dream had

included that I might have some of the conveniences that I saw in the catalog, such as electrical appliances that would make life easier and more comfortable. Our family has enjoyed these modern conveniences for many years. It had to be God's grace that watched over us and led us, to not only his eternal salvation, but also to many earthly blessings.

Perhaps I have another new beginning ahead of me as I prepare for one more move—to live with my younger daughter, Judy Aswell, in Bastrop. Life sometimes goes in circles, as that is where years ago I lived as a young single woman and then again when E.B. and I began our life with International Paper Company. Our children grew up there and attended school there. Both graduated from Bastrop High School.

Both girls married young men in the air force and traveled the world for many years. Linda was divorced and lived in Bastrop again for a short time before she remarried. She lived in several different parts of the United States, as well as Germany, Italy, and England. She has always loved traveling but has now lived in Camden for the past seventeen years. Judy lived in various places, including Alaska and Italy. Her husband, Eugene Aswell, retired from the US Air Force and became a teacher in Bastrop. She lost Eugene in January 2005 to a tragic accident. She and Katherine, her oldest daughter, still live in Bastrop where Katherine is a math teacher at Bastrop High. Her two younger daughters, Mary and Rebecca, recently moved to Kentucky for new beginnings. They each have dreams of their own and look toward following them. I certainly hope all their dreams come true as well as mine did.

Linda has retired from work and is helping me write this book. She has one son, Carl Edward Kitchens Jr., two step-children, and grandchildren of her own. Her granddaughter Suzanne Eliza is ten years old. She and her parents, Carl and Debora, live near us in Camden. I have had the pleasure to watch my only great-grandchild to this point become a beautiful young girl. Hopefully she will never experience the hardships that I had at her age. She will have dreams and challenges of her own in this new century.

Our world has changed so much since the time in which I was growing up. Looking back over the past eighty-one years, I certainly do not resent having lived through all the difficult times as a child. Each challenge taught me to be patient as well as grateful. Each one helped me to address later challenges in my life. Perhaps some people today do not know how to cope with challenges as adults because they were not taught the importance of responsibility as children. If children are given everything they want, then they are cheated of the joy of achievement.

At this point in my life, I feel that perhaps Judy and I can help each other as widows together. My health has been very good most of my life, and I am glad to be able to still be useful. Who knows what the future will bring for me? More challenges for sure. But through it all, my faith carries me and my Savior guides and loves me.

EPILOGUE

By Linda Duff Niemeir

Great-Grandpa Judy lived his final years in Mississippi with his older daughter, Iva. He died in 1951 at the age of eighty-seven.

Grandpa Clarence worked very hard most of his life as a sharecropper but was finally able to buy his own farm through a government program. He and Grandma lived on the government place near Boeuf River in Richland Parish about five years. Due to their health and age, my grandparents had to sell the farm, so he worked for a while at a dairy. Then in 1954 Grandpa had a stroke that left him paralyzed and incapacitated. He and Grandma moved to Bastrop, Louisiana, to be close to my parents, Lillian and E.B. Duff. Then Grandpa had a heart attack in 1957 and passed away. He is buried at Memorial Park Cemetery on the Crossett Highway north of Bastrop.

Grandma Eliza lived many years after that, first

with one daughter and then another and sometimes with elderly friends who needed help for a while. She went willingly to the nursing home when it became necessary because she did not want to be a burden to my mother. She went to be with our Lord and Savior in January 1992, at the age of eighty-nine, and is buried next to Grandpa in Bastrop. She has left behind a legacy of her Christian witness, as well as many lovely quilts and crocheted afghans.

My father, E.B. Duff, retired from International Paper Company in 1985 and lived many years on Upper White Oak Lake enjoying hunting and fishing. In 2000 he was diagnosed with Alzheimer's, so he and Mama moved to Camden to live next door to me the next year. Daddy had to enter a nursing home in 2003 and passed away in November 2004. He is also buried in the cemetery in Bastrop near the graves of my grandparents.

As for Mama's sisters, Aunt Margie Buffington is a widow and lives in Fruitvale, Texas, near two of her three daughters. Aunt Sue Metcalf lives with her husband, Leroy, in Choudrant, Louisiana, near two of their four daughters.

At this writing Mama is healthy and continues to sew, garden, quilt, and cook. She is still active at Chidester Baptist Church where she has been a member for over twenty-five years. She is now preparing for her move to live with my sister, Judy Aswell, in Bastrop.

As for me, it has been a special time this first year of retirement spending a lot of time with my mother, helping her write this book. She is a dear mother and a loving grandmother and great-grandmother. Everyone who knows her loves her and says she is special—and so talented! Not only does she sew, garden, and cook well, but she has written many Christian songs, painted many lovely oil paintings, made dozens of beautiful quilts and crocheted afghans. Most importantly, she is a beautiful Christian example. Mother has written some Christian songs, which you can find at my website www.niemeir-duff.com. You may print off the sheet music at no cost to you. Please feel free to use them, because God gave Mother the words and music to glorify his name. One of my favorites is "A Tribute to Mother," which was inspired by the life of my grandmother Eliza. Another favorite is "Children's Nature Song," which was inspired by my granddaughter, Suzanne.

Suzanne Kitchens, 5 years old in 2002